Inspiration 52

Inspiration 52

We all could use inspiration at
the beginning of each week!

Jerome Vincent Carter

Inspiration 52 Publishing
Long Beach, California

Printed in the United States of America.

Published by Inspiration 52
P.O. Box 17983
Long Beach, California 90807

www.inspiration52.org

Library of Congress Control Number: 2003103110

ISBN: 0-9725272-0-6
SAN: 254 – 9042

First Printing 2003
Second Printing 2004, revised
Third Printing 2005
Fourth Printing 2005, revised
Fifth Printing 2005, revised
Sixth Printing 2006, revised
Seventh Printing 2007, revised
Eighth Printing, 2008, revised

**This book is dedicated
to the life and memory of**

Freddie Carter

Josias Carter

Lloyd Carter

Aretha Carter

*A portion of the proceeds from
Inspiration 52 goes toward the*

*Inspiration 52
"Making A Difference" Scholarship Fund*

SPECIAL DEDICATION

This book is dedicated to the life and memory of these very dear students. They were here a brief moment but they touched my life and the life of others in a very profound way!

Ernest Dwayne Williams

MurJohnny Germany

Leonel Guzman

Frank Jimenez

Roy Jackson

*May we all be inspired
to make a difference on their behalf.*

Foreword

Inspiration 52 is an incredible collection of 52 contemporary, poetic, heartfelt selections with original quotes. The author chose the number 52 so that the readers can be inspired, motivated, and reflective at the beginning of each week throughout the year. This book is for teachers, CEO's, leaders, managers, coaches, laborers, administrators, professors, and any individual looking to be inspired. *Inspiration 52* comes complete with lesson plans for teachers. The lessons are tied into the California State Teaching Standards for reading, speaking, listening, writing, and social studies. The sections on **Inspiration** and **Motivation** are awesome, with such titles as: *I Have A Dream, Too; The Beginning; Today; You Are Your Brother's Keeper; Maturity; You Always Succeed When You Try; Be Yourself; and One Of These Days*. In addition, the **Reflection** section truly tells an insightful story from writer to reader. Just as King David wrote the Psalms and King Solomon wrote the Proverbs, these reflections are thought provoking and life changing. Titles include *Why Me?; Don't Make Excuses; It's Hard To Say Good-bye; What Is A Mother?; What Is A Dad?; What Does It Mean To Be Rich?; Material Things; What Is A Friend?; When Will I Learn?; and If My Life Were A Song*. The author feels that true reflection causes lasting change.

Inspiration 52 is a real winner! Rarely does a book of poems and quotes come along that has an immediate impact and impartation into your life.

The teaching tips and suggestions ensure that the poems and quotes will be maximized in their weekly usage and that poets will be developed and encouraged as early as kindergarten. Whether you use this book in the classroom, boardroom, or for your personal growth, your life and the lives of others will be challenged and changed for good. Yes, *Inspiration 52* truly lives up to its name. It will be enjoyed and appreciated by teachers, executives, leaders, coaches, students, and families for generations to come.

Preface

"I thought the poem, **How Do I Change?***, was written by James Baldwin or someone like that."*

Michelle Wills, Deputy Probation Officer
Los Angeles County Probation

"After I finished reading **Inspiration 52***, I was truly 'inspired.' What a wonderful collection of beautiful thoughts and encouragement. Thanks for pursuing your dream and in turn blessing others with what the Lord has given you."*

April Mosby, Educator
Lennox School District
Lennox, CA

"Mr. Carter, can I post **Chill On The Stereotype** *on my website?"*

Jerry Combs, Educational Assistant
Los Angeles County Office of Education

"Who writes the poems? Mr. Carter, really? Would you be available to come and share some of them on my television program?"

Carolina Castorena, Founder
CEO-Prevention Awareness Program
Los Angeles, CA

"Mr. Carter, **Don't Make Excuses** *is a tight poem. One of your best! You have to publish all of your poems!"*

Kawan Jones, Student
Crenshaw Community Day School
Los Angeles County Office of Education

"Man, you are just too deep!"

Tracey T. Carter, Educator
Long Beach Unified School District
Long Beach, CA

Acknowledgements

I would like to thank Dad and Mom who encouraged me to read and write at an early age. They taught me how to read and write before I ever stepped foot into a classroom.

To my wife, Tracey, who always encourages me to strive for excellence and will not let me settle for anything less!

To my five (5) brothers and two (2) sisters who always challenge me to be the best and reach for the stars. They truly give prophetic meaning to the title *Inspiration 52*.

To my father in the ministry, Dr. Billy G. Ingram, and my current pastor, Sheridan McDaniel; two men of excellence. Thank you both for blessing my life.

To my co-worker, Ms. Wills, for helping me notice that there was something special about my writing.

To the parent who asked in the middle of a parent conference, "Are you the one who sends home the poems?"

To my students, Richard and Kawan, who encouraged me to publish my poems.

To Marvin, the student who was always prepared to recite first in the class.

To my children, Jamaica and Jalin, who listened to Dad at the dinner table, smiled and said, "that sounds great," even if they thought it was corny.

Finally, to my one-year-old "surprise blessing" daughter, Jael, who is poetry in motion!

Contents

I. Inspiration

II. Motivation

III. Reflection

IV. Bonus Selections

V. Student Poems

VI. Thank You For Inspiring Me!

INSPIRATION

Inspiration or being inspired is the moment you realize that you have been called to greatness. It is that instant you are touched by someone's words, actions or life! At that particular time you understand that you could be doing so much more than you are doing right now! You then know that the sky is the limit and your mind and desire are the launching pads. The only thing left to do is to take steps toward your goal of making a difference in every life with which you come in contact. That's inspiration! Historical greats that have inspired me are: Dr. Martin Luther King, Jr., Abraham Lincoln, Harriet Tubman, Jessie Owens, Cesar Chavez, and Helen Keller, just to name a few.

I Have A Dream, Too

I have a dream, too
One day I hope it will come true

Family, friends, house, and a car
A career that takes me far

Doing what's right and nothing wrong
People of all races and colors getting along

Helping people to do better in life
I'll have 2 or 3 kids with a loving husband or wife

Earning respect because of the choices I make
Finally being real with myself, no longer a fake

Not trippin' on little things
Appreciating the happiness that life has to bring

Living life to the fullest because it is so short
Extremely thankful because I have a fresh start!

So, if this all doesn't sound new
It's not supposed to
Because I have a dream, too

■■

"Dreams become reality when I wake up and work."

<u>The Beginning</u>

Today is the beginning
And I have a feeling that I will be winning
A new chapter in my life opens while another is ending

Different setting, friends, and show
What's to come in the future, who's to know?

Since I'm here, I'll make the best of it
I have dreams and goals I haven't accomplished yet

I'll stay focused, take things one step at a time
Always try my best and things should be just fine

Be myself, stay cool, and show respect
These are life-long lessons I'll never forget

So, time to make moves, no need for pretending
Let's make good things happen
Since this is the beginning

■■■

**"If your future doesn't look bright,
make sure you're walking in the light."**

Today

Today is the day
That things will go my way

I'll learn and help a lot, things will go smooth
I'll get into a real nice groove
Everyone will get along cool

Things in the past will stay in the past
My future is bright, my positive outlook will last

Even if someone tries to bother me today
I'll ignore the small stuff and continue on my way

It's good to have at least one day
Go your way

All the other days, let's wait and see
Right now I feel it
Today has been designated just for me

It feels so good to smile and say
Today is my day!

∎∎∎

"Today is the moment and opportunity to prove and demonstrate the greatness that I have within!"

This Week

This week will be unique
It'll be the best in recent history

I'll accomplish much
I'll reach out to someone with whom I've lost touch

I'll try hard to do the right thing
Knowing the positive consequences it will bring
When I hear my favorite song, I'll start to sing

I'll keep the right attitude
I'll try hard not to be rude

I'm only responsible for me, so I won't make an excuse
It's time to grow up, besides, what's the use?

It'll start with me making an internal change
I've got a feeling this week won't be the same!

So, great things I'll expect and speak
Because my life won't be the same after this week

∎∎∎

"For seven consecutive days I will be prepared, productive, and profitable. Next week, I'll do it again."

What's Inside Of Me?

What's inside of me?
Am I all that I can be?
Is it something I want others to see?

Is it love, peace, honesty, or joy?
Bitterness, anger, hate, a scared little girl or boy?

Whatever is inside of me can't help but come out
It's time for me to figure myself out!

Two people seem to be at war
One trying to hold me back
The other trying to go far

I struggle to do what's right
But most times I lose the fight

I must focus on what I put inside of me
That's the only way to truly be free

Today I'll put love, peace, and truth in my heart
I think that's an excellent start

In the future, who am I to be?
It all starts with knowing what's inside of me

■■■

**"Who you are shows up when you're all alone
and think no one else is watching."**

How Do I Change?

Do I want to change?
Or should I stay the same?

Am I on the road that leads to productivity?
Do I understand that to achieve greatness,
 I must continue to improve me

What does life have to offer me?
With the right actions and attitude a bright future I can see

Should I make the change, and do and become the right thing?
It's important to remember, that through the change process
My composure and focus must be maintained

I ask the question:
What does life have to offer me, and how do I express my gift?
I now rephrase the question, and ask:
What do I have to offer it?

I know I can be great
So, if I'm to change, today must be the date

Enough time wasted, my life and priorities I will rearrange
This is how today I will make the change

▪▪▪

**"If you are unwilling to change,
you are refusing to grow and learn."**

Maturity

The definition of maturity
Explains all that you should want to be

It has nothing to do with number or age
But everything to do with how you behave

To be mature, you need several kinds of ingredients
You use words like discipline, responsibility, and obedience

Soon you must grow up
So the real you can show up

It has very little to do with what you say
But how you conduct yourself each and every day

So it's really up to you
To walk in a mature pair of shoes
Now the question is, what will you do?

Look around! Many people have failed to be all they could be
They had many things, but lacked maturity!

■■

**"Age is a number,
but maturity is my attitude plus my actions."**

You Brighten My Day

You brighten my day
Sometimes it's what you do
Other times it's what you say

It's a kind word, a smile on your face
You walk in the room and radiate the place

Some are a blessing when they come, others when they go
My life is enriched because it's you that I know

You could be a friend, co-worker, wife or husband
Boy, girl, man, or woman

The fact is you brighten my day
A part of my life, I hope you will stay

Fortunately for me, our paths have crossed
Without you in my life, I would be at a loss

I could go on and on because there is so much more to say
But let me sum it up by saying, you brighten my day!

■■

**"If you didn't make someone's day better,
does that mean you made it worse?"**

You Always Succeed When You Try

Never give up, that's not the way you win
It takes time and effort to be a champion

I will always try my best
Whether it's a game, interview, chore, or test
As of today, I will not settle for less

Soon all the hard work will pay off
And my dreams will come true, no doubt

There are no short-cuts to victory
My road to success must start with me!

I'm glad I have learned
That to be something in life it must be earned

Disappointments can make you laugh or cry
But I will remember, you always succeed when you try!

■ ■

**"All the times that I failed,
were the times that I didn't try!"**

The Sun Always Shines After The Rain

The sun always shines after the rain
Joy and healing does come after the pain

Restoration and redemption can come after the shame
If you lose today, tomorrow there's another game
Life can be sour, but it's also sweet as sugar cane

So shake the negative thoughts from your mind
If you look close enough, a silver lining you might find

There is a lesson to be learned in all we do
From this tough experience can come
Something fresh, exciting, and new

So it's not over, there's so much more to gain
Remember, the sun always shines after the rain

▪▪▪

"If everything in our life was always good, or went according to schedule, we would never have the opportunity to learn or grow."

The World Is Waiting For Your Gift

The World is waiting for your gift
So don't be selfish, share it and give society a lift

Don't be paralyzed by criticism or fear
You must understand, someone's life
Will be enhanced because you are here!

We all have special talents that we were blessed with from birth
To share, give and help others as we journey through planet earth

You have so much to offer this community
Whether it's artistic, writing a book or producing a CD

So, what are you waiting for?
Please don't procrastinate anymore
The world is waiting and there is so much more in store

Please don't say I'll wait to next year
Then you cheat the world for another 12 months my dear!
Don't let the thought of success or failure grip you with fear

Give your gift to the world and we'll celebrate and have a toast
You can make a difference or make excuses but you can't do both

It's time to prioritize, start the process and go down the list
Let the journey begin, because the world is waiting for your gift!

∎∎

**"Nobody can give your gift but you,
it's time to present the present!"**

<u>Keep It Real</u>

Keep it real
Regardless of how you feel

Don't say you will, when you know that you won't
Don't say okay I'll do it, and then you don't!

Don't build your life on things that are shallow and empty
Don't pretend to be for me, when you know you are against me

Don't walk around being a fake
Be honest at all times, no matter how high the stakes
Be genuine with people no matter what it takes

You don't have to lie to "kick it" or fit in
If you do, you need to find a new set of friends

Tell the truth when you are not sure what to do
What I guess I'm saying is, always be you!

It's not worth it to be a phony for others
It's always best to be who you are, that's what I've discovered

So let me say it again, so you will know the deal
And there won't be any question about how I feel
You get more out of life by being yourself and keeping it real!

■■

**"It's hard to be real,
when you don't know who you really are!"**

Know Fear!

Know fear
When it tries to appear

And tells you not to study from or write your own book
Or that you can't do something because of how you look

No longer let fear stop you in your tracks
For too long, you've let the unknown hold you back!

So why are you here?
To be consistently paralyzed by fear?
Check this out my dear!

Step a little closer let me shout in your ear,
so you can be sure and hear!
Today is the day that you recognize, organize, prioritize, realize
and get yourself in gear!

Someone greater than you has your back
Acknowledge fear for what it is, a bunch of crap

Open your eyes wide, leave the past behind,
no need to even look in the rear
Identify the problem, start moving forward
and tell your situation, I have no fear!

■■■

**"Fear is the opposite of faith and trust.
Of the three, fear needs to be eliminated,
the other two in your life, they are a must!"**

Somebody Saw Something In Me
That I Didn't Even See

Somebody saw something in me that I didn't even see
They not only saw me as I am
They visualized what I could possibly be!

My potential and all that I could do
I could make a difference in the world for me and for you

Become an entrepreneur or an inventor
Wow! Beyond the sky is the limit
I didn't see it but they wouldn't let me forget it

They encouraged me and pushed me to make the right choice
When I wanted to settle for less, I could always hear their voice

"Be the best, you can do it and do the right thing," they would say
Their motivation and inspiration
Helped me to get through many difficult days

Now I understand what they were trying to do
To get me to understand and realize
That I shouldn't cheat the world and myself, too

To believe in myself and impact the earth
To recognize that I was chosen for greatness before my birth

Now, looking back it's just amazing to me
That somebody saw something in me that I didn't even see

■ ■■

**"When you interact with others, don't just see the person, but
focus in on their potential."**

MOTIVATION

Motivation is the act of being moved out of your comfort zone into a realm of action. It is the ability to put feet and legs to all the ideas that have been swimming around in your head. Ideas that you have put off for too long, and let others convince you that you shouldn't or couldn't do. It is the act of going beyond complacency and compromise; to head in the direction of challenging yourself to change (for the better). Finally, it is to become a doer and not just a talker! That's motivation! People that have motivated me: Garret Morgan, Spud Webb, Doug Flutie, Jackie Robinson, Alice Walker, and Nelson Mandela, and the list goes on.

Be Yourself

Be yourself
Why would you want to be anyone else?

Choosing not to be yourself won't do
Because that will always make you number two

To try and be somebody else makes you second best
Which means in life you are settling for less

You are an original, don't become a copy
Because when you look in the mirror, you won't be happy

Even if others don't like who you are
Don't let them stop you from going far

Don't let them hate you out of the game
Just because they don't want to change

You have to be yourself, that's the only way to be free
Don't try to be him, her or me!

So when you look at your life
Like a beautifully framed picture on the shelf

Stand proud, smile, and say,
"I will always be myself!"

■■■

**"If you can't be yourself,
you make it difficult to be anything else!"**

I Can Do A Lot

I can do a lot
And I'm thankful for all that I got

I'm secure with who I am
Not trippin' on who I'm not

I can read, write, draw, dance, and sing
When it comes to self-expression, I can do almost anything

I have so many talents I've yet to display
Observe closely because today could be the day

In order to be great
I must stay focused because it's getting late

I want to do so much with my life
Own my own business, be a success, sounds quite nice

Many talents and gifts come from above
Not to mention many other things, including blessings and love

Now is the time to make a decision
Because I can do so many things with great precision

Even though over the years there were some things I forgot
As time goes on, I will be a success, because I can still do a lot

━━

"The more I do, the more I realize all the things I can do."

I Will Become A Success

"I will become a success!"
That is a phrase I will confess

Whenever I'm put to the test
I will always try my best
That's how I know I will become a success

Life is full of ups and downs
Hard work and a positive attitude can turn situations around

It's easy to give up and say, "Oh, well"
But with that perspective your destined to fail

Any great work was started one step at a time
Why should this be different, just because it's mine?

Everyday I will practice to go the right way
It's about what you do, not what you say

How bad do you want to succeed or start on your quest?
Should I be comfortable where I am, relax and rest?

No! I will work extremely hard, I won't settle for less
As of today, I will become a success!

∎∎∎

**"If you go through life without a purpose,
any path looks promising!"**

It's A New Year

It's a New Year
Is there anything I should fear?

I made some resolutions
Because in my life, I need some solutions

Some things I need to get right in my life
A New Year brings hope and the future seems so bright

It feels good to have a fresh start
A New Year, clear goals, and a clean heart

Who knows what a day might bring
How can you be so optimistic some may say?
Despite all that happens, I know that God brings the day!

This year is going to be great for me
I can go on and on talking about it, but just wait and see

12 months, 52 weeks, or 365 days
However you look at it
I'm going to be successful in so many ways

I'm looking forward to the unknown
With a smile, a laugh, and a tear
But it's all good because it's a New Year!

■ ■

**"It's a New Year, but the same old me,
unless I add discipline and courage to the recipe!"**

After This

After this, what's on the list?
Will I hit a homerun or swing and miss?

Will I score a touchdown
Or fumble and walk away with a frown?

Will I slam-dunk
Or commit a turnover like a chump?

Is my future really up to me?
I'll have to prove it can be

Can I walk on the road to success
If I always give life my best?

After this
All my blessings I don't want to miss

I have to get and stay on the right track
I refuse to let anyone or anything hold me back!

It won't be easy
But I know it's the right move for me

Starting today I'll focus, so don't trip
Because I'll be ready after this

■■■

**"The way you act speaks louder than what you say, so what
difference are you going to make today?"**

If My Life Were A Movie

If my life were a movie, who would play me?
Denzel, Tom, Antonio, Catherine, Julia, or Halle?

Would I be a villain or a hero?
Would I go up against Arnold or DeNiro?

It's cool to dream of being a star
This is just a thought, but I will go far

The movie would be great, everyone would go see it
It would be all about me. Wow, who could believe it!

Now I'll work very hard since this is the beginning
So I can be sure that my movie will have a happy ending

When I think about it, it doesn't matter who would play me
Not that I wouldn't be honored that my life became a movie;
But movie or not, in real life, it's only I who can be me!

■■

"If my life were a movie, would it be worth watching?"

If My Life Were A Book

If my life were a book
How would the cover look?

Would it be bright or
Would it be dark as night?

Would it be hard cover or paperback?
Would it be interesting or would it be wack?

Would I talk about the real
Or just write about something that makes people chill?
Hopefully, after they read it, they won't become ill

I would want to find the right words to say
To help someone have a better day

I'm sure my book would be a best seller
When you read about my life, you will find nothing better

My story would tell about "The Path I Took"
And that would be the title, if my life were a book!

■■

**"If my life were a book, would it inspire
or leave a lot to be desired?"**

**"If my life were a book,
would it be time to turn the page?"**

One Of These Days

"One of these days"
When it comes down to it, it's just a phrase

You must put action to words to get results
Don't be discouraged by put-downs, negativity, or insults

Keep moving forward, that's where the future lies
Not looking back, it's only memories behind

There is so much to live for along the way
Life is worth the living no matter what others do or say

A new day will come, that's not the issue
The question is what will you pursue?
Don't just talk about it, make your dreams come true

So snap out of your daze
Fight through the haze

Make your life more than a phrase
If your life were a book, now would be time to turn the page

You must do more than say
"One of these days!"

∎∎

"One of these days is an excuse, not an action."

Why Am I Here?

Why do I get up every day?
Why do I go to work, school, or play?

Is it to help others, or am I out for myself?
Do I hurt people, or do I offer help?

I ask myself, why am I here?
Minutes turn to hours, and days become years

I continue to ask hoping to find out
My life has meaning and purpose, but what's it about?

Today could be the day that the answer will appear
To the question asked most often, "Why am I here?"

■■■

**" 'Why am I here?' is a question most people chase,
but fail to catch, year after year."**

**"If you don't know why you are here,
how will you ever determine where you are going?"**

You Are Your Brother's Keeper

You are your brother's keeper
Which means you keep him out of trouble
Don't let him sink deeper and deeper

You watch out for him, and look over him
Be consistent even if you have to go out on a limb

And for your sisters, it's the same thing
Use all your efforts to bring them joy and not pain

A nobody can put anybody down
But will you encourage them to turn their life around?

It's easy to complain about what you've been through
But when you have the opportunity to make a difference
What will you do?

No need to blame society
When I need you to be there, will you be right by me?

Can I count on you to stop me from taking a wrong turn
Or will you let me self-destruct, crash, and burn?

You can make a difference, right now, today
Make up your mind and to yourself say:

"I will take ownership because prevention is much cheaper
As of this moment, I'm making it known
I am my brother's keeper!"

■■

**"Do you keep your brother out of trouble or in trouble? That
is the question."**

Be The Difference!

Be the Difference
Even when no one is there to observe, look or listen

Be the difference wherever you walk, drive or roam
Be the difference everywhere including school,
your job or at home
Be the difference even if you have to stand-alone!

Be the difference, live the example that you want to see
Be the difference for yourself, friends and your family
Be the difference, make a huge impact on society!

It all starts with making a decision right now
Telling yourself, I will be the difference in someone's life
someway somehow

So, with many others running from responsibility
It's obvious that making a difference must start with me

So, as I realize that my life has purpose and significance
I commit today to being the difference!

∎∎

**"Continue to be, and strive to become more and more,
the difference that you are looking for."**

The Game Is Not Over

The game is not over unless you quit
Get back up regardless of how hard the hit

The game is not over
I'm talking hard work, practice, and persistence, not a four leaf clover!

Luck has nothing to do with this
Planning, preparation and performance is at the top of my list!

I'm just in the half time of life
I need to make some adjustments, so things will turn out right

I need to stop making so many mental mistakes
Fumbles, air balls and turnovers are a result of going to fast and not
applying the brakes

The game is not over, it's only pre season competition
But I better learn the system of life, before I miss it!

Now this situation feels like a championship game
The pressure is intensified my composure I must maintain

To overcome this challenge I need focus, discipline and courage
When I apply the principles to my situation, my life will flourish

This is what I practiced so hard for, to prove myself in life
Now that it is game time, there is no place for fear, doubt or fright

No need to blame the official or the referee
He's there to keep order you see
The final out come of my life is up to me!

Now that I understand the rules of the game
A positive, productive, optimistic attitude is important to obtain

Whether I'm running down hill, sprinting, or climbing a boulder
I'll never give up or lose faith, because I realize, the game is not over!

■■

**"The game is not over, it's only halftime,
YOU must make the adjustment!"**

No Short Cuts

No short cuts
To be successful it will take courage and guts

No need for if ands or buts
Make the decision today to get out of your rut!

Resist the microwave solutions or the instant fix
Quick success pursued or gained will get you
into a strange mix

The short road taken
Will lead to a quick exit, with character and integrity
likely forsaken

Short cuts usually create a bigger mess
I've learned that the hard way I must confess

So save yourself some heartache, put forth the effort
and you will be fine
The road to good success requires a process and plenty of time

Start working hard, follow your dreams and never give up
Resolve in your mind to do things right and resist the short cut!

■■■

"Short cuts usually lead to a dead end!"

Doing Zero

Unfortunately, you are doing zero
And you expect to be treated like a hero

You have to make things happen and earn your dinero
When there is work to be done, locating you is like Finding Nemo

Nothing, nada and zip
Never constructive or productive, just a lot of lip

So, what should you do and where should you go
Let's start with a university, college or even a trade show

A seminar, workshop or a real-estate class will also help, you know
Discipline yourself and be assertive
That helps your creativity flow

We don't have time to be lazy, make excuses,
blame others and procrastinate
It's time to do more than zero before it's too late

Practice a lifestyle of commitment, perseverance and initiative
Stop begging and borrowing, get yourself in a position to give

Now is the moment and today is the day
to become your own superhero
Don't just exist, start living and
commence to do more than zero

ı■■

**"Success is no accident; it is directly related to planning,
preparation and perseverance!"**

Desire vs. Discipline

Desire combined with discipline
Is a formula that propels me to win

It is a must to have passion and desire
But without discipline, I won't climb much higher

Desire combined with discipline
Are two components that must come from within

I can talk and even dream about what I'm going to do
But if I don't discipline my mind and my body
My goals, aspirations and dreams won't come true

I need to turn off the TV, stop playing games and get off the phone
It's time to workout, do homework, create, invent
And keep my mind and body strong

Of course, no drugs, no gangs, no alcohol
No loser friends or misguided affection
Those distractions will take my goals and dreams in the opposite direction

To discipline myself is the toughest thing I've ever done
But without discipline, I don't know of any battle that has ever been won

Discipline must be combined with desire
Without them, life rolls along like four flat tires

I have the desire to sing, write, start a business and play ball
But without discipline in my life, there is no way I can give it my all

So, let me close with a message to family, students, athletes and friends
The only way to achieve greatness is to combine desire with discipline!

■■

"Your decision to discipline yourself, will determine your destiny."

Is My Microphone On?

Is my microphone on? Because no one is listening to me
I look around and what do I see

Gangs, drugs, alcohol, tobacco, temptations,
Distractions and violence
Check the volume, because I think my microphone is silent

Maybe what I have to say nobody wants to hear
Then I look at the faces of the mothers'
And I see a constant stream of tears

So, I have to believe what I am saying is relevant and necessary
Besides, if we continue to live like this,
The end result will be extremely scary!

If no one wants to listen to me, will someone else please speak up
We are losing a generation of youth and to stand by
And say nothing is very tough
Will someone join in and repeat after me, "Enough is enough!"

"Enough is Enough," now that would be
A good title for a hip-hop song
But before we begin to sing and record,
Let me ask you again, is my microphone on?

■■■

**"A silent voice can speak louder
than a shout from the highest mountain."**

Is The Richest Place On Earth The Graveyard?

Is the richest place on earth really the graveyard?
As I ponder this question, to give a response, it's somewhat hard

Think about it, many people merely exist from day to day
Paying bills, watching TV, living in mediocrity,
With nothing substantial to say

Spending valuable and precious time on things
And people that don't really matter
Never tapping into their legacy, purpose, or destiny;
Being content with idle chatter

Are you touching lives and impacting those around you
Your family, friends, community, state, country and the world too

Make your life count for something, today is the day
And the time is now
Get focused, develop a plan, don't procrastinate; stop asking how

So many people end up deceased with their ideas, businesses,
Talents gifts and inventions buried with them
You must start on your legacy today, take small steps,
Get a mentor; you must begin

Write your vision down, surround yourself with productive friends,
And start moving forward, it's not that hard!
Embrace your purpose and destiny because I refuse to believe and
Accept the thought, that the richest place on earth is the graveyard!

■■■

**"The seeds of greatness are deep within all of mankind,
waiting to be watered with a flood of hope, expectation,
encouragement, belief and faith!"**

Scared Straight Vs. The Challenge To Be Great

There was a time when you would have to tell the youth
About the dangers of drugs, gangs and jail
But in today's violent culture, our youth know those scenarios all too well

Someone in their family has been affected by
Alcohol, tobacco, gangs and other drugs

And a friend or family member has died a violent death
At the hands of a banged-out thug!

So the task is not to scare our youth straight
The goal is to give them hope, encouragement, love and the tools to be great!

I truly believe our young men and women want to do great things with their life
Own legal businesses, become teachers, coaches, doctors and lawyers
Start a family as husband and wife!

So let's talk to them and not at them, with honesty and compassion
It's time to eliminate this plight
We have to equip the youth with knowledge and wisdom
Along with the ability to choose right

We must dialogue and communicate before it is too late
No need to point fingers, fight, argue or debate
Prepare and produce solutions, now is the time and today is the date!

Because our young leaders don't need to be motivated
By threats or fear to walk on the path that's straight

Let's raise our expectations, our youth will rise to the occasion,
we must have faith!
Let's model love and hope as we give them the option and the
tools to choose to be great!

■■

**Intimidation and locking up our youth are
failed strategies of the past; we must equip our youth
with the tools to build a positive legacy that will last!**

REFLECTION

Reflection is when I sit still long enough to understand why I do the things that I do. It is to learn from my mistakes and the mistakes of others. It is to contemplate why things happen the way they do, and to know it is all for a purpose. It is to replay a situation in my mind and give it one hundred different endings. Then I ask myself hard questions and wait for answers before I move on. True reflection is to reconsider, re-think, revise, and revisit an occurrence over and over again in my mind while it is still fresh. Reflective thinking is to offer solutions and truth as opposed to complaints and criticism. That's reflection! Great Reflectors: Jesus Christ, King David, King Solomon, and C.S. Lewis, and many others.

Why Me?

Why me?
What was I created to be?

Why was I born into my particular family?
Why was I born rich or into poverty?
Why is it I have everything I want, but nothing I need?

Why is it I try to do right, but trouble seems to find me?
Why is it that I get caught, while others get away free?

Why do I think like I do?
Do others feel and think like I do?

Why do I act like I act?
I want to do better and that's a fact!

I want others to know the real me
But how do I get them to see?

This is a question that comes to mind constantly
I wonder if others ask themselves the question
Why me, why me?

■■■

" 'Why me?' should be rephrased to, 'it will be me!' "

Why?

Why am I black, brown, yellow, red or white?
Why does day turn into night?

Why do people I love tend to fuss and fight?
Why does it seem I can't do anything right?

Why am I short or tall?
Why does it matter at all?

Why am I young or old?
Why do I like the heat better than the cold?
Why can't I follow directions and do what I'm told?

Why did I do what I did?
Why can't I grow up and stop acting like a kid?

Why do I have so many questions?
Why does life have so many lessons?

Why do people lie, cry, and die?
Why, why, why?

■■■

"The 'whys' in our life make us bitter or better."

I Need To Slow Down

Every time I turn around
It seems something is going down

Things happen so fast
Accidents, celebrations, problems
The future is now the past

I need to slow down
Stop being a clown

No need to frown
Today is the day I will turn things around

Sometimes I don't even know where I'm going
So what's the rush

I need to appreciate the time I have with family and friends
Listen carefully and hush

Some refused to slow down
Some are six feet underground

I don't want to make that same mistake
So today, my time I will take

I'll watch the sunset
Take the time to appreciate things, I said I'd never forget

Listen to the birds whistle a beautiful sound
That's a great start because I need to slow down!

■■■

**"You have to take time to reflect on what just happened; even
a merry-go-round stops before it starts again."**

Where Am I Going?

Where am I going and how do I get there?
I think about the future and sometimes I get scared

Other times I'm going nowhere fast
I know what I'm doing now won't last

I need direction because my vision is blurry
Then I slow down and say, "What's the hurry?"

Help comes from above and within
So before I start my journey, that's where I must begin

As of today, I will be knowing
When I reflect on the question, where am I going?

■■■

" Why am I always in a rush to go nowhere fast?"

It's Hard To Say Good-bye

It's really hard to say good-bye
I think about good times and good friends and almost cry

Things won't be like this again
I'll look around and won't see certain friends
I truly don't want these special times to end

I'll only remember the good times
When thoughts of you come to mind

I've heard people say all good things must come to an end
But more times with these friends, I would like to spend

I know that time and change affects us all
Life sometimes bounces up and down like a basketball

So today I'll leave this place but not my friends
Relationships have been formed that won't easily end

I'll keep in touch and that's no lie
But I tell you the truth, it's really hard to say good-bye

■■■

**"It's hard to say good-bye,
especially if you don't intend on keeping in touch."**

Don't Make Excuses

What's the use of making an excuse?
Even if it's the truth, don't make an excuse

We all have to grow up some day
Excuses only lead to delay

Certain circumstances and situations we don't want to deal
But with ourselves, we must be real

Don't blame others if you don't reach your peak
To put it off on somebody else, that's very weak

I must look in the mirror and face myself
No excuses, I have to deal with me and no one else

So the question is what's the use
Of making an excuse?

Ask anyone who is a success and they will give you proof
The first thing they eliminated was an excuse!

■■■

**"If you keep making excuses,
you'll never grow up, only old!"**

What About The Pain?

What about the pain that frequently fills my brain?
What about the pain that makes me think I'm going insane?
What about the pain that occasionally pours like rain?

Because my dad or mom wasn't there
When I needed someone to care

What about the pain I feel because someone close to me dies
Or when someone I trust looks me in the eyes and lies?

How do I deal
When the pain I feel
Is so real?

How do I recover
When I've been hurt by yet another?

Step one: what's done is done
Step two: when I forgive, I begin to live
Step three: someone who cares, please help me
Step four: I'll begin to trust once more
Step five: I'm thankful I'm still alive

If I walk in these steps, a new opportunity I will gain
And that's how I will deal with the pain

■ ■

**"Pain doesn't discriminate, it will knock on your door
anytime and anywhere, no matter who you are!"**

When I Make A Mistake

When I make a mistake
How long will the apology take?

When I'm in the wrong
Do I make excuses that sound like a song?

Saying I'm sorry is part of being a woman or a man
I want to be treated like an adult, so this I must understand

Nobody's perfect, this I know
Why pretend and put on a show?

Making mistakes is a part of how we live
When I'm less than perfect, I hope others will forgive

Committing errors can affect your health
So when others forgive me, I must forgive myself

Life is awesome and delicate and there is so much at stake
But what we have in common is that we all make mistakes

■■■

"When I make a mistake, I can be humble and apologize, or I can blame others and hide!"

When Will I Know?

When will I know
Which way to go?

Sometimes I hear two voices
Helping me to make my choices

Which choice should I make?
I have to be careful, I can't afford another mistake

"Do the right thing," is what most would say
I know that's true, but should I obey?

It's tough with peer pressure surrounding me
If I were older, would I be free?

Okay, I'll make it a point to think before I act
That should help me make the right decision, that's a fact!

When I hear the voices saying yes or no
I'll make the correct choice on which way to go

■■

**"If you can't control yourself,
who do you want to control you?"**

My Life

My life has been full of ups and downs
Most times it evens feels like a merry-go-round

I guess I'm no different from anyone else
But in my mind, I feel like I'm all by myself

I'm not sure which direction I should go
At this stage in my life, should I already know?

So many places to go and things I haven't done
I refuse to be held back any longer by anyone

I need discipline to take control of my life
Work hard to reduce the stress and the strife

Is today the day I choose to do right?
Only I can answer that question because it's my life!

■■■

"Make the best of your life because after all, it's yours."

What Is A Mother?

What is a mother?
Someone who treats you like no other

She'll give you anything to help you along your way
Whatever it costs to help you out, she is willing to pay

Her love is so steep
Her heart is so deep
Her kindness is beyond belief

Her actions are selfless and true
Her goal and desire in life
Is to provide the best for you

She rarely complains
She takes things in stride and deals with the pain

Although she might have other kids
She makes you feel special no matter what you did

Moms are so much fun
You have yours, I have mine, we only get one

So, whenever you have the opportunity
Return the love she gave for free
Remember, moms are truly a different breed

Every lady is a woman
But some we classify as other

Through love, pain, and joy
They have earned the title Mother

■■

"Appreciate your mom while she is still here. If she has passed away, hold your memories and special times dear."

Why Should I Care?

Why should I care about anybody in here?
Why should I care about anyone out there?

Do I care about my family?
Do I show it by what they see in me?

Should I care about the people I meet and see?
Do I want people to care about me?

What's the point anyway?
Can I really make a difference in someone's day?

I'm sure I do, whether I realize it or not
Some of the bad examples I display need to stop

I don't think it's weak to show that you care
Deep down inside we all have those feelings to share

What's my next move?
Start being myself so my behavior can improve

So, the next encounter I have with someone
I'll stop, think, and stare
Then ask myself," Why should I care?"

■■■

**"If I can make a difference by caring,
shouldn't I make it a habit?"**

What Does It Mean To Be Rich?

What does it mean to be rich?
That someone should scratch whenever I itch?

That I go where I want,
When I want, and do what I want?

To walk around with a smile
That makes me rich now!

That I run my own show
Just because I have a lot of dough?

Should I give to the needy
Or keep it for myself and be greedy?

Should I give to the poor
So that poverty will be no more?

If I were rich, how much money would be enough?
Would I save some in case times got tough?

Would money change me like I've seen it do others?
Would I love it more than my sister or brother?

Right now some might say it's just a wish
But in the near future, I hope to experience
What it means to be rich!

■ ■

**"If I'm rich, does that mean I have great possessions,
or does that mean I possess the Greatest Gift of all?"**

Material Things

Material things
I'm still searching for the happiness
They are suppose to bring

I've got the house, car, and money in the bank
But I'm still not happy, why do you think?

I've talked to people with wealth and money
They are still searching for peace of mind and joy
Seems kind of funny

What does it take to be happy and how?
It's not in material things, I know that now!

So, day after day
I search and I pray
I'll continue to look above and within to find the way

Whether it's summer, winter, fall, or spring
I'm thankful I've learned
Happiness is not in material things

■■■

**"Is my goal accumulating material things,
or are they a benefit resulting from me reaching my goal?"**

Chill On The Stereotype

Chill on the stereotype
Because we all don't look alike

You judge me and don't know me, that ain't right!
You form an opinion about me because of how I look
That's not tight

Don't speculate, learn the facts
Get to know and observe how I act

You'll find I'm smart, intelligent, and cool
Now that you know the real me, do you feel like a fool?

Because I wear my pants baggy, you think I'm a thug
Or because I have large bills, I'm a criminal that sells drugs

Because I do or don't dress regal
You think I'm illegal

Too many movies and TV
Gave you the wrong perspective about me

So, let's start anew
And I'll tell you what we should do

For starters, don't believe the hype
That's how to chill on the stereotype

"If you form an opinion about me because of how I look, the clothes I wear, or how I speak, do I have a problem, or are you the problem?"

What Is Love?

What is love?
Is it something that comes from within, below or above?

Is it just for Valentine's Day?
Does it mean I get everything my way?

Is it bought, given or earned?
Everyone wants to be loved, when will it be my turn?

Love is something we all should give
It definitely helps us all to live

A kind word, a smile, I will give today
You know it's true what they say
The more you give, the more comes your way

Just like swimming in water, you're sure to get wet
The more you practice showing love, the better you get

Now that I think about it and focus my thoughts above
I realize, I have always been loved

■■

**"How is it we can attempt to search for something
we don't know the true meaning of?"**

Now That I'm Old

Now that I'm old
Do I remember what I was told?

Back when I was a kid
Do I remember the good and bad things I did?

When I get out of bed
Do I recollect all the things that have been said?

Did I make a difference in someone's life
By being mean, kind or nice?

What will my kids say about me?
Has my life been all that it can be?

What will be said when I'm gone, that I was wasted flesh
Or one of Life's best?
That I gave up too soon, or that I passed every test?

Will I leave a legacy
Or am I selfish only thinking about me?

When my name is mentioned, what will be told?
That remains to be seen, now that I'm old

■ ■

**"As I grow old, am I leaving a legacy,
or am I just leaving?"**

What Is A Friend?

What is a friend?
Someone that is there to the end
A person on whom you can always depend

An individual who won't let you down
Someone that can create a smile from a frown
When you need them no question, they'll be around

You go places, kick it and hang
They have your back if you ever need anything

A true friend keeps you from getting into trouble
When you need them, they are there on the double

If you are fortunate in life you might have two
True friends are hard to find and few

Would those close to you say you are a friend?
Someone with whom they would choose their time to spend?

So, if you have a friend
Whether it is a classmate, teammate,
Co-worker, husband or wife

Be sure you let them know
You're thankful their in your life

■■

"Do the people you call friends, consider you a friend?"

What Is A Man?

What is a man?
This is a question that few men understand

He should be able to conquer the earth
A natural leader by birth

He could be your husband, father, son or brother
A real man is like no other

Responsible, accountable, hard working, and kind
A genuine man is hard to find

A true man will always provide for his family
He will pay the cost no matter what the fee

Why are real men so rare and aloof?
They have chased a lie, to tell you the truth

The lie that they need something else to be complete
This lie has led many men to their defeat

The lie makes a man chase things he doesn't need
The lie confuses the issues of necessity and greed

The lie will have you trade family for prestige and money
This plight of most men is sad, not funny

A man has been made whole by a greater hand
Life would be easier if we followed His plan!

In order to be a real man
This truth we must understand

As a man what should I do?
Keep your focus above and with yourself be true

Immediately reprioritize, do all and the best you can
These steps start the journey
To the process of being a man

▪▪▪

**"If more men understood the process of becoming a man,
we would have less problems in the land!"**

When Will I Learn?

When will I learn
That if I play with fire, I'll probably get burned?

When will I discover
That if I do the right thing, greatness I'll uncover?

When will I know
That the truth must follow me wherever I go?

Will there ever be a time when I'll make the correct choice
And follow the right path when I hear that Still Small Voice?

Why do I do what I do?
One of these days, to myself, I'll be true

At this age, I should have learned from my mistakes
So, maybe I should closely consider the actions I partake

However you look at it, everyday is full of twist and turns
But today I ask myself again, when will I learn?

▪▪▪

**"Don't just focus on earning a living,
but concentrate on learning from living!"**

The Choices I Make

The choices that I make
Will determine the path that I take

If I take dope or drugs
I'll disappoint those that I love

If I join a gang
I'll bring my family pain and shame

If I hit up on a wall
A public defender or lawyer I'll have to call

Almost 100% without fail
If I'm hard-core gang banging, I'll end up dead or in jail

If I go to college,
I'll obtain a wealth of knowledge

If I get a job
I'm less likely to be a thief that has to rob

If I join the military
I'm sure to make others and my country proud of me
So, it's not difficult, but easy you see

Just like a baby that will crawl before it walks
And babble before it talks

Each step that I take
Depends on the choices that I make!

■■

**"My choices will chronicle my chances and my decisions
will determine my destiny!"**

If My Life Were A Song

If my life were a song
Would it be short or would it be long?

Would it be a cassette, album, 8-track or CD?
Would it be jazz, oldies, heavy metal, rap, classical or R&B?

Would it be real music or some junk?
Could it be bought in stores or sold out of someone's trunk?

Would my lyrics make sense?
Would it be thought provoking, or would it be dense?

Would I be compared to Marvin, Barbara, Mary J,
Luther, Diana, Tina Marie, Barry, or Michael J?

Who would be compared to me?
I hope not Milli Vanilli

Music is the best, it can help you relax and chill
It can make you feel better when you are ill

My song would be unique, it would come from the heart
And I can't think of a better place to start

If my life were a song, would it enlighten the nation
Or when people hear it, would they change the station?

The desire to know these answers are very strong
It's a very interesting thought: if my life were a song?

■■■

**"If my life were a song, would it be time to change the
station or would it be necessary for a total re-mix?"**

**"If my life were a song,
would I enjoy listening to the lyrics?"**

Who Am I?

Who am I?
I search the ground, I search the sky
But I'm often left wondering, who am I?

Sometimes I know, sometimes I don't
I feel that I'll find out, then I think I won't

I've been here a long time, but not long enough
To know who I really am, man that's tough!

The days come and the days go
I try to grasp who I am, but I'm just too slow

I ask others but they don't really know
The information I give them, it's just for show

So deep down inside, I look and I hide
For who I truly am, only I can find

Who am I?
Hopefully I'll soon find out
When I do, I'll live life to the fullest, no doubt

The toughest things in life can make you laugh or cry
Like honestly looking in the mirror and asking, who am I?

■■

**"Who you are eventually shows up
and lets others know all about you."**

What Is History?

Should history mean anything to me?
Sometimes history seems more like a mystery

Is it HIS-story
Or is it my story?

We all have a story to tell
Sometimes we succeed, sometimes we fail

The Indians contributed much and had their land taken
Africans were originators, sold into slavery and forsaken

The Chinese were doing well
Then dismissed from the country and expelled

The Europeans supposedly discovered
Something that was already there
And helped to establish a country that is unique and rare

The Jews were brutally mistreated during WWII
The Japanese were put into concentration camps
And asked America, "What did we do?"

History is full of ups and downs
Doesn't matter if you are white
Black, red, yellow, or brown

I'm part of it, so are you
Now what shall we do?

Represent ourselves well and be all that we can be
Because right now, we are making history!

▪▪▪

"What is history saying about me right now?"

Don't Judge A Book By Its Cover

Don't judge a book by its cover
Open it, you'll be surprised what you'll discover

It's hard to tell what's real by looking on the outside
When you get past the surface
You'll be impressed with what you'll find

Just like if you judge somebody by what they wear
Or stereotype someone because of the style of their hair

It's difficult to know what someone is about
When you don't know the inside, you only see what's out

The best book I've ever read looked plain on the exterior
But the content was quite superior!

Just like the finest people I've met
Looked like regular individuals at first glance, that you can bet

So be careful how you view one another
And always remember, don't judge a book by its cover

▪▪

**"If you judge something by appearance only, you are
cheating yourself from the best part."**

The Basket

Does anyone see or care about the man pushing the basket?
What about the youngster heading for or laid in the casket?

He was only in his teens
How did our hearts become so cold and mean?

Where did we go wrong?
We use to be a people that were so loving and strong

Now children are killed before birth
People, pollutants, and chemicals are destroying the earth

Babies are having babies
At times it seems the whole world is crazy

Wars and rumors of wars
Almost every night on the news, police are chasing cars

Is it America or is it the people? That's the question
Should we complain or go to confession?

How can we help Afghanistan
And ignore the plight of our fellow country man?

As I ponder this thought time after time
I'm reminded of the nursery rhyme:
"A tisket, a tasket…"

But I must change the words to:
"Does anyone see the man pushing the basket?"

■■■

**"If *you* can't change *in* your community,
how do you expect to change your community?"**

What Is A Dad?

What is a dad?
Someone I wish we all had

He takes care of the house and family
Goes to work, comes home, and is there for my siblings and me

Provides for mom and the kids
The home is safe and secure because of what he did

Runs and handles his own business, plus goes to work
Always kind, loving, and real, never acts like a jerk

If your dad passed away
Let us have a moment of silence
And a prayer we'll say

If your dad wasn't there, then he missed out
The joy of raising a family
Is an incredible accomplishment without a doubt!

Nothing can take the place of a family
Not a temporary feeling, fortune, fame, or tons of money!

So we take time to say thanks to a man who is also a Dad
We appreciate you being here through the good and the bad

Hopefully one day I can look in the mirror and be glad
That I have become the answer to the question,
What is a Dad?

■■

**"If more men that had children were actually dads,
the world we live in would not be as sad."**

Now I'm Dad

Now I'm dad
And I'm both glad and sad

Now that I'm dad it means that my dad has passed away
It was unrealistic but I was hoping that as a part of my earthly life
He would always stay

He was the greatest man that I've ever known
He always made sure our house was a home

Now my children call me dad
It's an awesome responsibility
But it's also the best feeling I've ever had

Being a husband and a father
Is the most incredible thing that I've ever done
There are plenty of good days but some days are not exciting and fun

Some days are difficult, challenging and tough
But that's all part of being a real dad;
You take the smooth with the rough

It's humbling to look into the faces of my kids and my wife
Then I think to myself, what a wonderful life

So daily I commit to rise to the occasion
And give my family all that I have
Just as my dad did for me, until I take my last breath,
I'll embrace being called, "Dad!"

■■■

**"D-A-D; when used properly, they are three of the most
powerful letters ever used in the history of mankind!"**

Is Life A Test?

If life is a test
Then I should always try my best

I hope to pass and not fail
What are my options, freedom or jail, stay or bail?
Are the stakes higher, as in heaven or hell?

The important thing is not to cheat myself
By putting forth an effort, I can gain knowledge and wealth

Some days the test of life is okay
Other times I don't know if I can make it through the day

If life is a test, what's the final reward?
How do I know if I got an A, B, C, or D on my report card?

Better yet, who gives the grades?
I guess I'll have to wait and see
But as Tupac said, "Only God can judge me."

These are some hard questions, I'm not sure of the answers
Just like in life you might experience
Success, rejection, healthiness, or cancer

Then there are times
When I know things are going to be just fine

Other instances, I don't know if I'm traveling east or west
But I still search for that elusive answer to the question,
Is life a test?

**"If you can't pass the test in the classroom,
how do you expect to pass the test of life?"**

Life Is An Open-Book Test!

Life is an open-book test
You must try your best

The answer is in front of you
Focus, work hard, be patient and make your dreams come true

There is no way you can fail unless you give up
Remember, the book is open; you can prevail, even when things get tough

There are no tricks or gimmicks in an open-book test
Put forth the effort, why would you cheat yourself and settle for less?

Take your time and read closely what life is teaching you,
It's all right there
Maintain your poise, it makes all the difference
When you are confident and prepared

The exam is daily and it occurs over a lifetime
The interesting aspect is, you have your specific test and I have mine

The answers to life are all around you and me
The book is open, just follow the plan, the information is free

Don't give up and don't compare yourself to others
Our exam books are different, that's what I've discovered!

So, get to work and don't be discouraged by exams of the past
It's a new day, this book is open, and it's a totally different class

You have a second chance that most people only dream about
Now you have to move forward, there is no room for fear or doubt

You must demand 100% of yourself, until you are put to rest
Keep in mind; life is a beautiful journey, as well as an open-book test

■■

**"Life teaches us and we learn. Life teaches us and we must not forget.
We teach others with our life and we must never forget that!"**

Why Do We Hurt Each Other?

Why do we hurt each other?
Is it because I don't respect my sister or my brother?

Is it because I don't know who I am?
Is it because I don't understand the Master's plan?

Why do we put each other down with the words that we say?
Wouldn't it be easier to help someone along the way?

There is so much evil around us
What can I do to not get caught up?

I really hope I can help the people that I meet
But I'll need courage to accomplish this feat

Today, I'll show unconditional love
Towards my sister and brother
And stop asking the question, why do we hurt each other?

■■■

**"When you rob a people of their true history and culture,
they have nothing to talk about except each other."**

If I Were God

If I were God
Now that would be odd

Everyday I would see babies born, people being married
Not to mention those being hurt, killed and buried
When you think of it, that's very scary

But I could also help and protect a man, woman, or child
By just moving my hand, now that would be wild

I wouldn't have to eat or sleep
I would regulate the entire universe and not miss a beat

Everyday would be different, there would be so much to do
For every age group, gender, race, religion, and color, too

To will, to deal, to heal
Sometimes to watch and sit still

Everyone would depend on me, the entire universe I would run
Even before something happened, I would know the outcome

The more I think about it
I have trouble buttering corn-on-the-cob
So I'll continue to be myself, and let God do his job!

■■

**"How could I run the universe
when I can barely balance my checkbook!"**

When I Die

When I die, will anybody cry?
Will they remember me for the truth or a lie?
Will my new home be below or in the sky?

What about the great things I've done?
Will they fade like the evening sun?

What will be remembered most?
The crazy things I used to boast?

The humorous things I would say
To help pass the day?

What will be important to me then?
Money, fame, family, or friends?

What did I work so hard for?
To feed the hungry or give to the poor?

To save all my money
Of which I can spend no more?

Now that I'm gone
Will my family be all alone?

And better yet, where am I?
I guess only God will know the answer to these questions
When I die

■■

**"Death, the common denominator
in this equation called life."**

Thank You

Thank you
But whoever knew?

That I would be here today
To express my gratitude in such a way

To family, mentors, teachers, homies, and friends
So many things to thank you for, the list would never end

But I hope you realize now
That who I am would not be possible
Without your encouragement and comfort, no way, no how!

The challenge and push not to give up
You told me to keep looking above
Even when times got tough

The smiles, hugs, or handshake you gave
Maybe it was an admonition, reprimand, a wink or wave

I say thank you because it all worked together for good
To do it all over again, of course I would

We had fun, we worked, we laughed, we joked, and we cried
We pulled together when a baby was born or someone died

Most would be fortunate to have one friend in life
But I'm exceedingly blessed to have you all
Three kids and a loving, beautiful wife!

So, let me stop here because there is still work to do
But please, let me say it again
Thank you, thank you, and thank you!

**"The road to success may be less traveled,
but the journey can never be accomplished alone."**

Who Knows?

Who knows what is going to happen today?
Who knows what some one might do or say?

Who knows what the future will hold?
Who knows what secrets someone has been told?

What shall I do next year?
When will my destiny appear?

What shall I do now?
Can I be successful and how?

Who knows who's next to be outlined in chalk?
Who knows where we will be placing flowers and a candle on
the sidewalk?

Who knows the difference between a raven and a dove?
Who knows why there is too much hate and not enough love?

Who knows why trends, traditions and fads will come and go?
All of these questions to whom do I bestow?
Will some one give me some answers, so I can stop asking,
who knows, who knows?

■■

**" The paradox of life, full of questions,
yet filled with answers."**

If I Knew Then What I Know Now!

If I knew then what I know now
Life would be different some way some how

Some places I would or wouldn't go
I would learn to relax and take things slow

Certain actions I wouldn't partake
Some people that aren't here I would show more love
and truly appreciate

I would strive to improve my integrity and stop being so fake
The road less traveled I would definitely take

If I knew then what I know now
I would focus on what's important, many distractions I wouldn't allow

My family and friends I would show much more love
I would seek to find my purpose by looking above

I wouldn't waste so much time chasing material things
I wouldn't think that the only way to be important was to achieve
fortune or fame

I would let the whole world know, that by helping others
is how you really gain
For all my mistakes, excuses and even successes I take all the blame!

Yes, I've learned some valuable lessons in my few years of existence
Others go their entire life and still don't get it

There are no regrets, life is good, you live and you learn
It builds character as you go through life's twist and turns

As I ponder and reflect all I can say is," Wow!"
Because I know my life would be different,
if I knew then what I know now

■■■

"Everyday is an opportunity to be better and wiser than the day before."

Life's A Trip

Life's a trip, where will it take you?
And as you venture through life what will you do?

Do you value it like a precious stone?
Do you realize you are here on a loan?

Do you appreciate life every day?
Or are you waiting for something or
someone to be taken away?

We've all had to deal with an illness, birth, marriage, divorce,
death and much more
As the day turns to night and night to day, what else is in store?

A triumph, victory, disappointment or setback
Every day it's a challenge to keep your focus and stay on track

You get a letter, e-mail or phone call and it seems that your life
is thrown into the abyss
Nevertheless, I'm thankful as I walk this journey trying my
best not to slip
And time after time I'm reminded that life is a trip!

■■

**"As unpredictable as life is,
it's still a blessing to be an active participant!"**

The Mirage

Things aren't what they always seem
At times it's hard to tell what's real and what's a dream

There are material things that we work so hard for
Then we obtain them and want them no more

It really seems odd
But life reminds me of a futile mirage

It's like a body of water in the middle of the desert
But it's not really there, my mind is reacting to the hot weather

Such is life as we seek and we find
What's real and what's a mirage, I don't know half of the time

How much effort do I put into the mirage?
Do I really own my home and the car in my garage?

Eventually does it all just fade away?
Which makes me a pilgrim trying to find the true way

As life moves on I still feel very odd
Because it reminds me more and more of a deceptive mirage

■■

**"If all of this eventually passes away,
then why work so hard for things that won't stay?"**

Am I Sorry Because I Got Caught?

Am I sorry because I got caught?
And with all that just happened what lessons have been taught?

Would I still be doing the same thing if nobody found out?
Does this incident reflect what my true character is all about?

Am I sorry because what I did was wrong?
And if I wasn't exposed, the question is, how long
would the behavior continue to go on?

Is it a relief that I was busted?
Now I can move forward and once again be trusted

"I was going to stop anyway,"
I'll look in the mirror and to myself I'll say

No one knows how this deception was allowed to start
And no one knows if I'm truly sorry, because they can't see
my heart

You can only imagine the inner struggles and mental
altercations that I've fought
And now, I'm not even sure if I'm sorry,
just because I got caught!

∎∎

**"If everything done in the dark eventually finds it way to
the light, then why do I deceive myself night after night?"**

The Games Are Over

The games are over I'm not playing anymore
I'm getting older and wiser, I know for me there are
better things in store

There was a time in my life that growing up was a challenge
But now I realize my life I must manage

Since I'm through playing games
Some of my friends and places I frequent I must change
Some habits, vices and priorities are deleted and rearranged

It will be difficult and tough
But after years of faking and shaking, enough is enough

It seems that some people never want to change
So their motives and existence are to play immature little games

I see why some people are successful and others are not
It's the 18 inches between your head and your heart

Some only want to be plastic, shallow and waste time
Others understand that to be mature requires a renewing of the mind

No need to apologize, explain, buy flowers or cry on my shoulder
I don't mean to be short but put away the letter and close the folder
Today marks a new chapter in my life, let me make it clear,
the games are over!

■ ■

" Let the games end, if I really want to play,
I prefer chess or dominoes with a real friend!"

Am I Happy With Me?

Am I happy with me
Am I pleased with what I have come to be
When I look in the mirror do I like what I see?

Does everything I touch turn to gold
Or does it begin to look and smell like mold?

What in my life do I need to change
What attitudes and behaviors do I need to rearrange?

How do I treat others, am I respectful, courteous, bossy
Courteous, loyal or trustworthy
I need to evaluate myself to know what's inside of me

What issues in my life do I blame others for
Knowing that in the majority of circumstances, I'm at the core

I need to take responsibility for me
And everything that I am and will come to be

So I sit, ponder and wonder what could be
Because my future success begins when I answer the question
Am I happy with me?

■■■

"The problem is not always someone else, it could be me."

The Mirror

The mirror tells no lie
I look at myself and say hi and bye

I never look long enough to know who I am
When I think about evaluating me, I hurry and scram

Who am I, what's inside of me and where do I go?
If I look in the mirror long enough, I'll be forced to know

So, I dodge and hide
I'll wash my face but I won't look inside

I'll brush my teeth
But past the surface of my flesh, I won't dare look beneath

I'll even clean my skin
But to examine my motives and my heart, I'm afraid to look within

So, I remain plastic and shallow
Because who I am, I don't even know
And when I'm around others I put on an incredible show

For all the acting I do I should win an academy award
But honestly, my pretending prevents me from moving forward

So, today the end of my hypocrisy draws nearer
I will have the courage to do more than maintain my hygiene
When I look in the mirror

■ ■

**"If the mirror is a true reflection of me,
then I must ask myself the hard question, do I like what I see?
And better yet, am I pleased with what I am growing to be?"**

Why Did We Have
To Graduate From Grade School

Why did we have to graduate from grade school?
Life was good and everything was cool

Childhood was great
The only worry was little league baseball practice, don't be late!

Everybody was still alive
My favorite group, no question, was the "Jackson – 5"

We rode bikes, skateboards, went camping,
Played ball and swam during the summer
To be on punishment in June or July, now that would be a bummer!

Going back to school in September, that was even alright
In December, in anticipation of Santa, we stayed up all night

We walked to school in the rain and the cold
We weren't concerned about arthritis or getting old

No bills, no mortgage, no rent and of course no debt
Just do your chores, your homework, be in before
The streetlights come on and take care of your pets

I miss those times, my dad and mom, my two sisters and five brothers
It was arguably the best time of my life; it has been like no other

So, as I reflect and remember how life was
All about following the "Golden Rule"
I ask myself time after time,
Why did we have to graduate from grade school?

**"Times and seasons change, but relationships,
if wisely and properly maintained, can remain."**

Broken Toys

There are so many broken toys
Disguised as young girls and young boys

I see them everyday
It breaks my heart in many ways

They also look like teenagers
Whose parents for many selfish reasons have become strangers

Now the children are left to figure life out
The result is broken toys and shattered lives without a doubt!

The broken toys grow up to be women and men
And the cycle of broken toys starts all over again

I know it is extremely important to take care of the planet and study the
weather
However, it's more important to invest in our children and keep families
together!

Please, let's study global warming
But the rate of divorce and teenage pregnancy is quite alarming!

Think about this, you and I could be broken toys because of what our parents did
So does it make sense to have children and then allow them to become broken kids?

So how can we prevent the cycle of toys from being broken again?
By asking mom and dad to stay married to the end

By showing them the silent anger, frustration and devastation of a broken toy
And how the self-sacrificing love between a husband and wife
Creates a beautiful world for a girl and a boy

Our children deserve the best including a life and family filled with joy!
It's our responsibility to stop this repeated selfish cycle of creating broken toys!

▪▪

**"Children need a real dad and mom more than material things;
kids desire love and quality time and then we will see a change!"**

Things Money Can't Buy!

There are things that money can't buy
Which will give and bring you joy, when you may want to cry

When the economy seems to be falling apart
That's a good time to examine your heart

Money is necessary; of course, I know this to be true
But if earning money is the reason for your existence, you have a lot of
maturing to do!

Money can buy a house, but it can't buy a home
It can't buy true friends to communicate with, but it can buy a phone

Money can buy fake friends who smile in your face when they are in need
However, money can't buy the unconditional love of friends and your family!

Money can buy associates, but it can't buy trust
Money can't buy love, but it can buy lust!

Money can bring you wealth
However, money can't purchase you a quality life and guaranteed health

Character, Integrity, Class, Peace of Mind, Courage, Humility and Self-Control
Are things money cannot buy; so never make money your ultimate goal

Knowing your purpose in life and who you really are…
With no money in your pocket can take you extremely far!

Contrary to popular belief, a large bank account
Is not the most important thing in a person's life
Serving others, meaningful and productive relationships and walking in purpose
Are intangibles that are far above any price

Hopefully we learn the truth and prioritize our lives before we die
Some have learned the hard way; the most important things in life money can't buy!

■■■

**"Life itself is priceless;
It is worth more than anything you can put on a price list!"**

BONUS SELECTIONS

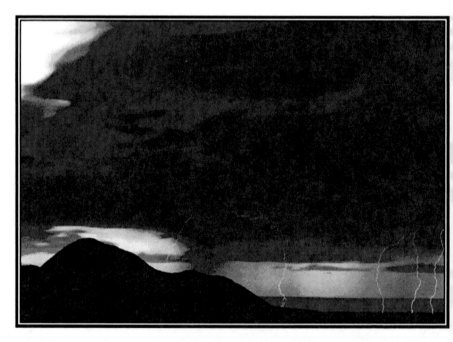

Inspiration 52 was intended to be a book of 52 poems; however, when you are inspired to write, you have no choice but to do what you love to do. As a result, and for your benefit, I hope you enjoy and appreciate the additional writings.

What Is Christmas About?

What is Christmas about?
At what age do you really find out?

Have I found out yet?
When I learn the truth, will I forget?

Is it about giving or should I take?
Am I real with people or am I a fake?

Showing love and concern one day of the year
That's kind of weak, my dear!

Is it about me and my list?
Is this the true meaning of Christmas?

Should I give love on that day?
Shouldn't I do this anyway?

Isn't it about a gift given from above?
Isn't it to celebrate His grace and His love?

One day I will know without a doubt
What Christmas is truly about!

■■■

**"Am I still asking what did I get,
or have I begun to ask, what can I give?"**

Holiday Season

Oh, how I love the holiday season
To call family, friends, and loved ones
It gives me the reason

Christmas, Hanukkah, Kwanzaa, or Thanksgiving
It's good to be in decent health, grateful, and living

To let those close to me know I care and I'm near
To reflect on the blessings and grace of the past year

To see the kids that have grown so tall
To enjoy good food, desserts and all

To say thank you and share hugs and a gift
To encourage my brother or sister and give them a lift

To let them know that it's going to be okay
Even in the darkest night, morning brings a new day

Oh, the holidays are special indeed
Remember it's about love, peace, and joy
Not hatred, envy, and greed

So, as the year comes to a close, maintain focus on the reason
Be sure to make that visit, call, and show love
Because it's the holiday season!

▪▪▪

**"The holiday season is the time of year
that we are reminded that family, friends,
and relationships are what's truly important!"**

What Is A Teacher?

A teacher is a special kind of creature
They come with many special features

Some days they maybe a doctor or lawyer, take your pick
Other days mom, dad, friend or psychologist

Sometimes they actually get to teach
It should be everyday but there are many needs to meet

As teachers, we do so many things
Counsel, teach, break up fights, all before the bell rings

We all remember that special individual
Who helped us reach our full potential

Teachers love to show their students the way
We look forward to the *beginning* and *ending* of each day

We can assist a misguided soul that's gone astray
No one will ever say that we do it for the pay

We even educate at a sporting event while in the bleachers
Why? We smile and say, "It's because I'm a teacher."

■■■

**"A teacher is someone who comes
to work everyday prepared to make a difference."**

"We all teach something to someone everyday!"

Thanksgiving

What's so special about Thanksgiving?
For starters, I'm grateful to be living

Number two
It's great that I have positive people in my life, like you

Number three
All right, give it up for the dressing, desserts, and turkey!

Number four
The future has many blessings in store

Number five
Can't wait to see all the family and relatives arrive

Number six
Hope mom and grandma make my favorite dish

Number seven
Everyone should be here at half past eleven!

Number eight
Let me stop writing so I won't be late

Number nine
Feeling even better as it gets closer to the time

Number ten
Next year, I'll be even more thankful to do it again!

**"One thing that I have learned along the way is that
every morning I wake up it's *Thanksgiving Day!*"**

To My Wife

To my wife
A beautiful lady to which I commit my life

Everyday will be our day
Great memories and special times
We'll create every step of the way

Between us there has always been lots of love
This trend will continue, that you can be sure of

I wanted to take time and let you know
There's plenty of love that I've yet to show

The friendship, favors, and fun have just begun
As I walk by your side, the lottery I feel that I have won

I need to say thank you for sharing my life
And remember, that I will always love you as my wife!

**"To journey through life with a friend who is also your wife,
definitely adds blessings to a man's life!"**

Increase The Peace

Please, let's increase the peace
From South Central Los Angeles, to New York, Europe,
Africa, and the Middle East

And every city, state, or country that's in between
Let's focus on interventions, solutions, and tranquil things
Eventually, it will foster a more positive scene

Whether it's Compton, Watts, Manhattan,
Pakistan, Ireland or Iran
Someone needs to develop a peaceful plan

A suicide bomber here, a scud missile or drive by there
Acts of violence and terrorism affect families everywhere

We all have felt the pain and hurt
Of following someone we love in a hearse

Regardless of race, color, nationality, religion or age
We need assistance from above in order to end the rage

If we want a better life for our children and future generations
We should strive for peace in each and every nation

So, I'll say it again, last but not least
We better make it a point to increase the peace!

■ ■

**"If we don't strive for peace everyday,
then the world as we know it will pass away!"**

Relationships

Relationships, wow, this topic is daring!
An understanding between two people
To be loving, friendly and caring

To commit, compromise, to be trusting and true
That's a huge responsibility for me and for you

Is there another way?
Deceiving, cheating, selfishness, you might say
The pain that it causes is a high price to pay

Not to mention you've hurt someone
And possibly ruined their life
Doesn't matter if it's a friend, co-worker, husband or wife
Take your relationships seriously at all times, day or night

Starting from elementary, middle or high school
A good, positive, and productive relationship is quite cool

Be wise and don't take them for granted
Some have and regretted it while remaining on this planet

When your relationship is over and gone
Dig deep inside, find the strength, and move on

Be extremely careful of what you let roll off your lips
Knowing that whether it's good, bad or ugly
It will have a lasting affect on your relationship

■■■

**"When you understand that your relationship is like a
precious jewel, you *will* guard it with your life!"**

You Never Know

You never know which way the wind will blow
You never know if the day will go fast or slow

You never know who will be here today and gone tomorrow
Always be prepared to smile, give a hug and say hello
Don't hold back, let all the love in your heart show

Time is too short to be petty and hate
Don't hesitate! Forgive and truly forget, before it's too late

Once someone is gone
They can't smell the flowers or receive a call on the phone

Then you spend time wondering what could have been
Instead of appreciating the company of family and friends

So think about how you treat people
What you do and where you go

Because you can be with them today
And tomorrow, you never know!

**"Since it's difficult to predict the future,
make sure you carefully plan your present!"**

I Apologize To Myself

I Apologize To Myself
For putting my brilliance, talents and integrity on the shelf
For living like I don't have access to greatness and wealth

For not being a leader and following the crowd
For acting ignorant, undisciplined, loud and wild

For destroying my body and my mind with alcohol and drugs
For pretending to be something I wasn't created to be, a gangster and a thug!

For running from inspiration, love and hope
For not studying to my ultimate potential and acting like a dope

For running from the truth and living a lie
For putting myself in dangerous situations, and accelerating my chances to die

For talking too much and always thinking I'm right
For suppressing my intelligence and not acting bright

For abusing my body with foolishness and bad choices
For listening to haters and liars and not the right voices

For choosing Losers as my so-called friends
For not being true to who I am, and always having to pretend!

I apologize to myself, for too long, ME, I have robbed!
For acting mean, impolite, indifferent, rude and odd
For embarrassing my family, myself, my people and my God!

Now that the apology has been accepted, rise up and make up for lost time!
No need to feel sorry for yourself; it's time to shine!

Please Don't Get High!

Please don't get high
Because like smoke, your dreams will blow away in the sky!
Not to mention, it will eventually destroy your mind and you could even die

When you are getting high
You are kissing your hopes, dreams, motivation, inspiration and memory good-bye

Even if you say, I'm only going to do it once; it could be your first and last try
It will lead to homelessness, poverty and addiction; add to the list, you will live a lie!

Trust me, you don't want to be that girl or that guy!
It's guaranteed that all those who truly love and care about you will definitely cry

Stay away from weed, kush, alcohol, 8-ball, methamphetamine, X, crack or coke!
Prescription drugs are just as bad, they kill your brain & body and that's no joke!

Please don't get high!
It won't help your life soar or fly

And if you are drinking or abusing alcohol
You are setting yourself up for a major fall

It breaks my heart to see my community destroyed, devastated and decimated
because of drugs
To see members of the community incarcerated as if they were animals or thugs

To see someone treated as if they were inferior to a rodent or a bug
They've lost total control of their life and have to sleep under the freeway on a rug
Because they thought it would be cool to do alcohol or drugs

And let's not forget what has happened to so many families
When the parents have lost sight of their priorities

And decided that drugs and alcohol are more important than the children or baby
I don't have to tell you, it is one of the most pitiful & pathetic sights you'll ever see!

I've written many poems, some make you laugh and some make you cry
However, this is a serious message from my heart to yours, please don't get high!

Getting high is a waste of time and a waste of your mind!
Don't believe the lies; getting high will not make you cool. On the contrary, it will
turn you into a fool!

88

Waiting To Die

I saw a group of young men standing in front of an apartment waiting to die
One of the youth confessed to me that he was sorry that he believed the lie

He felt that he cheated himself and felt he wanted to cry
He remembered when he was in grade school he had dreams that soared beyond the sky!

He also admitted that this was prior to him getting high
Now he is just kickin it with no motivation, struggling to get by

He said, I actually forgot who I am
Now my entire existence has become a sham.

At one time I was brave, bright and brilliant as a light!
Played sports, was extremely creative, and could always read and write
I'm not joking, my game was always tight!?

Now I sit in front of the spot with the homies, waiting to die
Some are strapped with the burner; it's just a matter of time before the drive-by

Soon the hood will be washing cars, holding back tears trying not to cry
So let me say it now, bye-bye!
Because I refuse to change my life and leave this corner,
I'm just waiting to die!

It is unfortunate that we have believed and internalized the lie,
that all we can do is destroy and terrorize our own community and wait to die!

Master Peace

If the world is to survive we must Master Peace
If the human race is to stay alive, we must Master Peace

To stop all the wars
We must Master Peace

To prevent people from getting locked behind bars
We must Master Peace

To eliminate criminals from jacking cars
We must Master Peace

Why do people who look, breathe and bleed the same, hurt and kill each other?
Because we haven't Mastered Peace

Why do people betray their own biological child, mom, dad, sister or brother?
Because we haven't Mastered Peace

Los Angeles, New York, Egypt, Chicago, Houston, Miami, Palestine, Korea, Iraq,
Iran, Afghanistan, Pakistan, and Israel
What's the Deal?
We Must Master Peace!

Domestic violence, gangs, drive-bys, lies, deception, bullies, cyber bullies,
government cover-up and corruption
What a Beast!

So what's the Answer?
We must ask the *Prince of Peace* to help us Master Peace!

"Just a piece of peace in every heart will eliminate 99% of the problems before they
start!"

Live Like You're Dying

Live like you dying
Truly forgive and don't pretend to be trying

Learn to be a giver and stop the compulsive buying
Practice being real with others and stop the lying

Tomorrow is not promised nor guaranteed
Stop being governed by vanity, hatred and greed

If you only had 24 hours left to live, what would you do?
Are your relationships based on things that are noble and true?

Just imagine if you only had a week left on planet earth, and this you know
Would that affect the way you treated others and where you would go?

Would you be wild and reckless destroying everything in your way?
Or would you be humble, loving and reflective, and all the laws you'd obey?

Shouldn't we live like we are dying everyday, inside and outside our house?
Maybe we should be nicer to our friends, family, kids and our spouse

So, stop making excuses and really start trying
No matter how you look at it, we should live like we are dying!

"We should live like we are dying because one day we will be right!"

What's Cool?

I always had troubling distinguishing exactly what is cool
Then I attended the graduation at the local school

I saw one kid that couldn't participate in the ceremony wearing a frown
Then I realized he was the same kid that acted as the class clown

I saw kids receiving certificates trophies and making speeches
They were the students giving so much to the school, not the leeches

I saw parents proud of their son and daughter's accomplishments
That's cool

I saw parents crying tears of joy
That's cool

I saw students being recognized for their hard work
That's cool

I saw students receiving their certificates because; they had been accepted to college!
That's cool

I saw teachers proud of their students because they accepted the challenge to be great!
That's cool

I saw principals and administrators proud of their entire school!
That's cool

Don't let anyone lie to you as they try to encourage you to act like a fool
Acting smart and being intelligent are the keys to success.
That's Cool!

"Too many times we let losers define cool! Ask someone who is doing the right
things with their life to explain to you what's really cool!"

Being Tough vs. Having Courage

Brothers, we must talk about the difference between being tough and having courage
We must understand the difference if our families and communities are to flourish

Being tough says, "I'll make you a baby's momma, abandon you and the kids and ruin your life."
Courage says, "I'll be patient, court and date you and make you my wife!"

Being tough says, "I'll do a drive-by and shoot up my community and try to kill."
Courage says, "I am my brothers' and sisters' keeper, and in my community I'll teach, cultivate and heal."

Being tough says, "I'll rob you and take what you have so I can buy something I really don't need."
Courage says, "I'll get educated, work and earn my money and refuse to focus on vanity and greed!"

Being tough says, "I'll be selfish, narcissistic, immature and only think about me."
Courage says, "I'll be here through the good and bad times, I'll stick it out and never abandon my family."

Being tough says, "I'll put on an imaginary mask, medicate myself with alcohol and drugs and pretend this is the real me."
Courage says, "I'll be sober, strong-minded, vigilant and never alter my mind or body to escape reality!"

Being tough says, "I'll talk mean to a woman, punch, kick and slap her in the face."
Courage says, "As a real man, I'll never put my hands on a woman in anger because it's a complete disgrace!"

Being tough will have you front like you are credible, lie, steal, cheat, fabricate and use a fake name
Courage will have you be real with yourself, stand proud, be responsible and take all the credit or the blame

Being tough gets loud, ignorant, makes a scene, makes excuses and blames others
Courage is responsible, disciplined, humble, patient and always looks out for his sister and his brother

Now, look deep inside, stop acting tough and start living with courage
I guarantee your life will change and your hopes and dreams will start to flourish!

"Make no mistake, acting tough and having courage are not related. They are complete opposites, no need for this topic to even be debated!"

Face On A Program

As I look down from above, I saw my face on a program
I wondered if the picture accurately displayed who I am

It captured me on a day that was one of my best
Now on this particular day, my body is being laid to rest

I know it's a fact, one day we will all have our face on a program
So I need to make my life count, so it won't be considered a sham
I must live with integrity, because eternal life is not a joke or scam

As I looked down from above
I saw people greeting each other with so much love
I thought, shouldn't we treat each other like this every day, with love and hugs

I saw people I said I was going to call
They were laughing, talking, crying and embracing in the church hall

I saw people who said the were going to call me
I guess that's a call I won't receive

I saw people who I didn't expect to be there
It took something like this for me to realize, they really did care!

It's tough to say goodbye to my friends
But to our earthly existence, this is how it ends

As the service proceeded, I was in the casket alone
Just like everyone else, life after death, is a journey we must travel on our own

So my recommendation is to get your life right because eternity is not a sham
One day, just like me, your face will be on a program!

"As you view my remains, know that it is just a shell. My spirit is above in heaven
doing extremely well."

Greatness Doesn't Discriminate!

Greatness doesn't discriminate
However, it does require sacrifice so get busy and don't procrastinate

It's time to get focused before it's too late
Greatness doesn't discriminate, but if you're not serious about life it won't wait

Pursue greatness as if it were your ultimate fantasy date
Greatness by your side for life is an awesome mate

Order greatness from the menu and consume every morsel off the plate
When others ask how you did it, tell them from greatness you ate

Explain how they can do it too, renew their mind and they too can participate
Digest the principles and concepts, apply them to your life so you can become great

No excuses climb the wall, jump over the fence or leap over the gate
Nothing can stand in your way but _YOU!_ Because greatness doesn't discriminate!

"How long will you blame others for where you are?
Taking personal responsibility for your life, is a road that will take you far!"

Inspiration52 August 2011©

95

Stop Playin'

You can be sailing along in life whistling, skipping, laughing or praying
Then you feel like you've been hit in the stomach with a sledge hammer and all you can say is, "Stop playin'"

Here are some examples of what I'm sayin'
You can relate because you have heard yourself say these exact words, "Stop playin'"

I got a call this morning; they told me my best friend had died in his sleep
Then I received a voice mail, text and an e-mail that my homie had been shot in the streets

My family called and said our uncle has cancer and he will live maybe a few weeks
I received a pink slip from my employer, stating that my job I could no longer keep

Highway Patrol calls and says your family has been involved in an accident and the car is in the creek

At first, I began to panic and my knees got weak
Life hits you so fast and the future can seem quite bleak
You get hit on the same side of your face twice, even before you can turn the other cheek!

You try to take life one day at a time, but now you're not sure if you can make it through the week!
Before you can focus on one problem, you're hit with another situation before you can speak!

So you close your eyes, meditate, get quiet and start prayin'
Then you form your lips and utter the familiar phrase, "Stop playin'"

"Sometimes life feels like you are a part of a stage performance and everyday the director changes the script."

The Outs

I was in my old neighborhood and I saw an old friend. He was brilliant no doubt
But as we talked further, I noticed somewhere over the years he had lost his clout

He confessed that he refused to grow up and be a real man, and started to pout
That's when, he left his wife and children and walked out

He said he became friends with the wrong crowd and this is what he talked about
He told me he was:

Just getting out
Had been smoked out
Cracked out
Burned out
Bailed out
Ran out
Banged Out
Kicked out
Turned out
Sold out
Played out
Drugged out
Bought out
Found out
Called out
Choked out
Stomped out
Rained out
Carried out
Put out
And
Left out

It made me want to cry in frustration and shout!
It was obvious he had cheated himself over the years without a doubt

Now he's looking for a hand-out
Then a funeral procession passed us by, (the kid was only 16), what's that about
Makes me doubt if we will ever be able to pull ourselves out

But I refuse to lose hope, because we can:
Get out
Stay out
Help out
Pray out
Be about
Dream about
And live life to the fullest with no doubts!

"Let's help out, so we can have less misery to talk about!"

97

It's Not Halloween But You Are Wearing A Mask!

Preventing others from learning in the community or the class
Never being the real you, afraid to complete a simple task

So many offering help and solutions, but you refuse to ask
Now you are faking like you are tough, getting ready to be put on blast!

Instead of being a winner, you are acting like a loser and will finish last
Your life has been played with Monopoly money, never real cash
Instead of talking about something productive, you consistently talk trash

Or, some might say it this way
When describing you, I've heard them say

You are wearing your mask and it's not Halloween
Talking loud and putting up a front, being heard, before you are seen

It's really kind of sad that we have to pretend that we are mean
Living life on accident, not having the courage to get serious and follow your dreams

Either way you look at it, you better change before you crash
We've seen it before, how your life will self- destruct, because you want to act brash
It's hard to live life, when it's not Halloween, but you insist on wearing a mask!

"Take off the mask and be who you are. Despite what you say, you're being a phony
for others and it's dimming your star!"

Inspiration 52 August 2011©

98

Behind Closed Doors

Behind closed doors, there is always a different story

And for most of us, once the doors shut there is not much glory

We pretend to be one way in public, but at home that's not what we display

We talk a good game away from home, but in the house we are ashamed of some things we say

Ask the people we live with about the things that are heard, but rarely seen

It's like most people are wearing their mask and it's not even Halloween

It's very disappointing to see so many that are private failures, but a public success

When will we make our families a priority, live the truth, and give our spouse our best!

Behind closed doors, some strange things have taken place

Then you see the person the next day, and they tell you they are doing fine, with a straight face

How can you hit your wife and curse out your kids and be nice to others that are not your family

Go to work, do your job, laugh and smile, but at home you're considered the enemy

It's not fair to your family, but you continue to put up a front and live a lie

Instead of love and peace, your home is filled with tears, fear, intimidation, anxiety and a constant cry

So let's be real behind the closed doors, because our kids don't need to see us live a double life

Enough of the mixed messages; it's time to model integrity for our children, husband or wife

I'm not impressed with the title, position, cars, house, job, vaulted ceiling and the hardwood floors

My heart is broken for those who live in fear, because of the awful things that happen behind closed doors!

"Why live a lie? Have courage and be real with your family; stop trying to impress him, her and everyone else you see.

Celebrate and Then Elevate

Celebrate today and then elevate tomorrow
Go to college and beyond, get the scholarships and try not to borrow

We are so proud of you, but it is only the beginning
One chapter of your life is opening as another one is ending

Elevate your thinking, there is no limit
Dream big, discipline yourself, make correct choices and go after it!

Start planning your encore, your show is not over
This is not only a stepping stone, it is like hurdling a boulder!

As we look into your eyes, it's obvious that the best is yet to come
There is much more to accomplish, it's where you are going, not where you are from!

Keep striving and reaching higher, don't let anything or anyone hold you back
Do the right things, stay focused, surround yourself with greatness and stay on track!

Be sure and thank all of those who helped you get to this incredible day
You can use their encouragement as fuel as you continue on your way!

You have accomplished much and in the future the whole world will call you great
If you choose to accept the challenge, to celebrate and then elevate!

"Celebrate and then elevate. Don't be complacent with your current state; because there is a place waiting for you, it's called Great!"

The Homies, The Haters and The Hood

The Homies, the Haters and the Hood
These are entities that can be ugly, bad or good

I've seen people thrive and survive while dealing with all three
I've seen the 3- H's prevent many people from becoming all they can be

Don't get caught in a trap, use the 3-H's as fuel to not let anything hold you back
Color is no excuse either, no matter if you are brown, white or black

The Homies, The Haters and The Hood
Are 3 things that don't always function as they should

But I refuse to let anything or anyone hold me down
I won't let Haters prevent me from owning my own business or town

I won't let the Hood define who I am
I won't let the Homies turn my life into a sham

I'll think for myself and make the choice that is right for my life
I'll recognize how intelligent I am, I'm gifted, unique and extremely bright

So watch your steps and live life as best as you could
And don't be distracted or limited by The Homies, The Haters or The Hood!

"In life there are many things that can hold you back and take you off track, but
stay focused and do all that you should. Beware of The Homies, The Haters and The
Hood."

STUDENT POEMS

When students are challenged to look deep inside themselves to see what's there, you get amazing results! They put pen to paper, take a risk to express their thoughts, and create the following masterpieces!

My Brother's Keeper

Am I my brother's keeper? I'd say yes
I encourage my people to always try their best

If I'm my brother's keeper, who will be the keeper of me?
Or will I get sucked in by society?

I will be my brother's keeper even when times get rough
And help him hold his head up when life gets tough

When times change and if I notice my people getting weaker
Let it be known I will always remain my brother's keeper!

Written by
Michael Penn, 11th grade student, Crenshaw CDS

If My Life Were A Song

If my life were a song
It would probably be long
It would reflect on my life and make me strong

If my life were a song, it would probably be on CD
Influenced by Nas, but written by me

My song would be considered one of a kind
As you listen to it, it'll only get better with time!

As time goes by, whether it's right or wrong
It makes me wonder about if my life were a song

Written by
Michael Penn, 11th grade student, Crenshaw CDS

The Sun Always Shines After The Rain

The sun always shines after the rain
So take the good with the bad, the joy with the pain

Life sometimes seems like a rainy cloud
It follows you wherever you go

Just hold on through the bad times
And the good ones will surely flow

So, no matter if it is a storm, earthquake, blizzard or hurricane
Just remember, the sun always shines after the rain!

■■■

Written by
Kawan Jones, 12th grade student, Crenshaw CDS

<u>The Basket</u>

When I see the man pushing the basket
It reminds me of teardrops and a closed casket

Some of the men pushing the baskets had kids and wives
And some are looked upon as wasted lives

Looking at what society has brought
Some students in classrooms with the wrong things being taught
Death has become more of a reality and less of a thought

Some predicaments in life are often drastic
So why does everyone overlook the man pushing the basket?

■■■

Written by
Michael Penn, 11th grade student, Crenshaw CDS

What's Inside Of Me?

What's inside of me?
I know things I can't see
I can't even think of what it would be

I hope that it's good
I'm thinking it really should

I hope it doesn't turn out to be bad
If it is, I'm going to be mad

I remember my dad ran away like a hound
But it's cool, I did frown, but now I don't want him around

His loss, he made a mistake
I'll be sure to ignore his shoes, those steps I don't want to take

I know I'm not going to make my son mad
Because I'm going to be a great dad!
And he's going to be glad

As I look deep within, I don't know what it could be
But until I know, the question is, "What's inside of me?"

■■■

Written by
James Clavon, 10th grade student, Crenshaw CDS

The Choices I Make

As a child
I was young and wild

I didn't care about nothing
My granny always told me to become something

I did things to get attention
All I was looking for was love as my definition

Mommy and Granny were there
Daddy left, he didn't seem to care

Getting kicked out of every school
Disappointing Granny, that wasn't cool

As a little girl I was doing my thang
My family ignored me, so I began to gang bang

I woke up and said gang banging wasn't for me
To drown my pain I started drinking and smoking weed

I got tired of wasting time and throwing up
So I said now is the point in my life where I need to grow up

Now I'm in school doing well and not acting crazy
In the future, my plans are to go to the Navy!

■■■

Written by
Jami Burrell, 10th grade student, Crenshaw CDS

Now That I'm Old

Now that I'm old
My story of life, I've never told

Negative things I'll never do
Because I'm me and will always be true

Following all directions from Mr. Carter
After achieving much success from Crenshaw Learning Charter

I want to thank others who believed in me
And finally, I'm able to set my life free

With this final speech that I've told
And ending with the title, "Now That I'm Old"

∎∎

Written by
William Savery, 11th grade student, Crenshaw CDS

Why Am I Here?

Why am I here?
The day I find out hopefully is near

Is it to complete a mission or task?
I have so many questions but who do I ask?

Time is moving fast and we are getting old
Thinking back on when I was a kid
Respect your elders is what I was told

What does life really have in store for me?
I need to know my purpose and destiny

I live life with love and no fear
And hopefully I'll find out why am I here

■■■

Written by
Kawan Jones, 11th grade student, Crenshaw CDS

Why Do We Hurt Each Other?

Why don't we love each other?
Maybe because we don't respect each other
Or because we need a man in our life called a father?

When I respect my sister and brother
We will learn to love each other

I really hope to get respect in life
Then my life will soar as high as a kite

If you give respect, you'll get respect
But if someone gets out of line, they'll get checked

Please do what you have to do, but don't kill each other
So I can stop asking the question, "Why do we hurt each other?"

■■

Written by
Lamar Chapman and William Savery
11th grade students, Crenshaw CDS

My Life

My life can be very crazy
Thankfully it's been very good lately

I just checked into this school
I think it's very cool

My life is getting better everyday
I stopped listening to all the negative things
People have to say

I've started to do the good things I'm suppose to do
My life looks bright, it is not through

I will do my best
Until I'm put to rest

My mind is right
My game is tight

I will fight to the end
Hopefully, I'll always have money to spend

This is my life
It's as sharp as a knife
I have a feeling everything is going to be all right!

■■

Written by
Earnest Williams, 12th grade student, Crenshaw CDS
October 10th, 2002

111

Inspiration 52 Pledge

I will recognize and live like I know and
believe that I am gifted, talented and unique
beyond anything that I can imagine.
As a result, I must be accountable to those
in authority and take full responsibility for my actions.
I will always work hard doing the right things,
because this is how my dreams will come true.
I understand that my choices
will determine my ultimate destiny in life.
I understand that I can persevere
through pain and tough situations.
I will make a sincere effort to get along with others
because I recognize that no one succeeds alone.
I will learn from my mistakes and participate
in events that will move me forward in life.
I am a leader.
I am Inspiration 52!

What is the most significant point of the pledge? Please explain why
this point is so significant!

_____
_____
_____
_____
_____
_____
_____
_____
_____
_____
_____
_____
_____
_____
_____
_____

Write your own personal pledge to yourself!

_____
_____
_____
_____
_____
_____
_____
_____
_____
_____
_____
_____
_____
_____

The Power And Beauty Of Choices

Your choices are the dots that will connect your future and create a picture for your life! Everyday you make a choice to connect the dots of your life. What image has your choices created for you today, this week, this month, this year? Please explain:

Your choices are the pieces to your puzzle that will come together and create a scene of your life! What does the finished picture look like? Give specific details! Can you complete a puzzle without looking at the picture on the box? How?

Your choices are the clicks of a camera that you will take over time that will develop and create a series of moments that will display your life!

Your choices are the strokes of a paint brush on a canvas that will create a portrait that is your life. It is our hope at Inspiration 52 that your portrait will be a masterpiece!

Your choices are like steps on a staircase that will lead you to a destination in the present and in the future. Write the direction your steps are taking you in; are you pleased with the direction you are going? What do you need to do to continue on the right path or what do you need to do to change directions?

_____
_____
_____
_____
_____
_____

Your choices are like pages in a book that will publish the autobiography of your life. How can you make sure your story has a happy ending?

_____
_____
_____
_____
_____
_____

Your choices are like a video camera that will produce the movie that you will star in! How did you movie start? How will it end?

_____
_____
_____
_____
_____
_____

Your choices are like lyrics to a song that will play in your mind throughout your life for your enjoyment or regret!

The Power of Choices Reflection Questions

1. Which scenario do you identify with the most? Why? Share your answer with three other people in the class or group.

_____

_____

_____

_____

_____

_____

_____

_____

_____

_____

2. Create three scenarios that are not listed. Work with one of your peers if necessary.

(A)_____

_____

_____

_____

(B)_____

_____

_____

_____

(C)_____

_____

_____

_____

Suggestions/Tips For CEO's, Leaders, Managers, Coaches

- Select a poem or quote.

- Apply the poem or quote to your team/company philosophy.

- Have employees discuss or write how the poem or quote ties into a particular theme, i.e. teamwork or interdependence, or win/win situations or whatever your focus is for the meeting or seminar.

- Ask thought-provoking questions. How does this poem or quote relate to your job description or position? How does it help with the employees that you supervise? Does it have any impact on how you deal with your superiors? Could this poem or quote have an effect on your work habits or attitude in the work place?

- Have employees find poems and quotes from this book that tie into the goal(s) of the company/organization. Have them memorize and post it at their workstation or desk. This will serve as a constant reminder to keep working for the betterment of the team/company.

The Twelve Principles of Success

Teachers, these twelve principles were piloted with various students for two-and-a-half years. The poems were used to reinforce the principles. The results were incredible. Attitudes and behavior changed for the better. The students began to talk about purpose and destiny in their lives. The classroom became a team and a community of learners that genuinely cared about each other. It was truly encouraging to see the principles being implemented into the students' daily lives and they didn't really know it. They just began to live it! Wow! Now that is what every teacher lives for, to make a difference and to help encourage lives to change for the better. Well, the twelve principles of success are here to help you do just that. To make a difference in the lives of many or as the poem states, "Be The Difference!"

Inspiration 52

Twelve Steps of Inspiration, Motivation, Reflection and Education - Principles of Living

Principle #1 - You have a special gift to offer to the world. Recognize it, understand it, cultivate it, and give it.
Poems - Be Yourself, The World Is Waiting For Your Gift, Be The Difference, Somebody Saw Something In Me That I Didn't Even See

Principle #2 - We are responsible for our actions and ourselves. We will not blame others for what we do.
Poems – Don't Make Excuses, One Of These Days, No Short Cuts, Keep It Real, Am I Happy With Me?

Principle #3 - I will always try my best at whatever I do. I will make a positive difference and be productive.
Poems – You Always Succeed When You Try, After This, The Game Is Not Over, If My Life Were A Book, Desire vs. Disciplne

Principle #4 - Positive choices usually result in positive consequences; negative choices lead to negative consequences.
Poems – The Choices I Make, What's Inside Of Me?, How Do I Change?, When I Make A Mistake, Doing Zero

Principle #5 - You must consider your future with every choice you make. A victorious life is a result of making consistent, correct choices in life.
Poems – I Will Become A Success, I Can Do A Lot, If My Life Were A Song, The Games Are Over

Principle #6 - You must always dream big; never limit yourself.
Poems – I Have A Dream Too, Know Fear, If My Life Were A Movie, Don't Judge A Book By It's Cover, Thank You

Principle #7 - Without maturity, you will never develop the patience or persistence to be a winner!
Poems– Maturity, Why Me?, Where Am I Going?, My Life, What Is A Man?, Who Am I?, Is Life A Test?, If I Knew Then What I Know Now, You Never Know, The Mirror

Principle #8 - Regardless of how bad things might look, they will get better!
Poems – The Sun Always Shines After The Rain, Why?, The Basket, Who Knows?, Increase The Peace, Thanksgiving

Principle #9 - We must always look out for each other regardless of race, color, ethnicity, age, disability or gender. The most important race on earth is the human race.
Poems – You Are Your Brother's Keeper, You Brighten My Day, Why Should I Care?, What Is A Friend?, Why Do We Hurt Each Other?, Relationships

Principle #10 - We all deal with pain. It helps us learn, empathize, and grow. If things always went the way we wanted, we would not feel the need to change, develop or achieve greatness.
Poems – What About The Pain?, It's Hard To Say Good-bye, Chill On The Stereotype, What Is History?, When I Die, Life's A Trip

Principle #11 - When I learn from my mistakes, I'm able to help myself and others!
Poems – When Will I Learn?, The Mirage, Am I Sorry Because I Got Caught?, I Need To Slow Down, What Does It Mean To Be Rich?, Material Things, Now That I'm Old

Principles #12 - Today is the day I will choose to change. It's my decision! It's my destiny!
Poems – Today, The Beginning, This Week, Why Am I Here?

Inspiration 52
The Importance Of Teachers Who Care
Are You Aware Of Who You Are?

1. You teach more than just academics and the arts. You teach **who** you are through every encounter you have with a student.

2. You are more important than a brain surgeon. A surgeon can only operate on one brain at a time. You operate daily on at least 20 or more brains at the same time.

3. You are as noteworthy as a president that runs a country; you run a classroom, which could nurture the next president of the United States.

4. You make more than any CEO could ever make. You **make** students realize their ultimate potential. You **make** them reach beyond the sky and become great!

5. You are more valuable than any athlete that entertains for millions and shuns being a role model. You are a role model that does not require millions to know that you make a difference each and every day.

6. You design more than an architect; you design a system of success for your students that will encourage them for a lifetime.

7. You build more than the greatest contractor; you build hopes, dreams, character, integrity and values.

8. You are more significant than a pilot that carries passengers from one destination to another in a matter of hours. You carry students from day to day for months at a time, higher and farther than any plane can ever go.

9. You create more than any artist or poet; you create living masterpieces.

Jerome V. Carter
Inspiration 52 © April, 2004

Inspiration 52
The Importance Of Teachers Who Care
(continued)

10. You are as vigilant as a soldier defending a country; you defend someone whose   world would fall apart without your support, encouragement, and protection.

11. You are more important than an investment banker; your returns and dividends will be paid in ways that are priceless.

12. You are more critical to a community than a real estate developer creating a shopping center. You develop a vision of the future that will affect lives and generations to come!

Teachers, these 12 comparisons are written just for you. No one really knows what it's like to be you. The effort and sacrifice that you make on a daily basis is incredible. You play more roles than an award-winning actor in a full-length production. Your students depend on you in more ways than you'll ever know! Be encouraged your hard work is recognized, valued and appreciated.

So, in honor of you I compared you to several other professions, 12 to be exact; however the list could go on and on. No other profession could compare to what you do daily. Please accept my small token of appreciation. I hope it will be a constant reminder that you are one of the greatest influences in the life of your students! Be Inspired!

Suggestions/Tips For Individuals

- Select a poem or quote that applies to your particular situation or circumstance.

- Write down the poem or quote to reinforce its meaning. Create a reflective journal of your favorite poems and quotes. Write what they mean to you.

- Memorize the poem or quote. Post it on your bathroom mirror, refrigerator or desk.

- State it daily as an affirmation until you see a change or it becomes second nature to you. For example, the quotes from the poems entitled: *I Have a Dream, Too; I Can Do A Lot; The Choices I Make; When Will I Learn*.

- Ask a friend to hold you accountable to make the change or to help you improve upon your particular situation.

- Encourage and inspire others by sharing what you are doing and accomplishing.

- When you complete the process with the poem or quote, find another one and start the process again.

- E-mail the author and share your ups and downs, setbacks and successes, your mountain top experiences and valley lows (jerome@inspiration52.org).

- Keep a positive attitude and take it one day at a time! Smile, take time to laugh, and read your poems and quotes while you are watching the sunset or a waterfall, or simply walking on the beach!

Words Of Wisdom From The Author

- Keep a balance in your life, remember to truly appreciate family and friends.

- Life is too short to hold grudges. Be the first to forgive others (even if they don't forgive you). Most importantly, be sure and forgive yourself.

- Take time to laugh at yourself, it's okay. Most events are not life or death situations.

- Develop your character, not necessarily your charm.

- Increase your integrity, in addition to your intelligence.

- Keep your heart pliable, not hard like a rock or stone.

- Information without application is nullification. This means you must apply what you know and learn to your life or it can't help you!

THANK YOU
FOR INSPIRING ME

Every now and then people touch your life and you never have the opportunity to say thank you. Rarely do you seize the moment and tell them that you love and appreciate them. Well, here is my chance to say just that!

Thank You For Inspiring Me!

During my lifetime I have had the pleasure of interacting with all of you, which in turn has inspired me to produce such a work. I cannot thank you enough for your continuous support as I go through this journey called life!

My beautiful wife Tracey, who has encouraged me to be the best for the past 28 years. Freddie and Artina Carter (father and mother), Josias Carter, Lloyd Carter, Lavel Carter (my hero growing up), Aretha Joshua, Maria McClendon, Freddy Carter, Leo Carter, Dr. Billy G. and Solombra Ingram, Mark and Niecy Watkins, Ms. Freddie Gieger, Dr. Harriet Williams, Dr. John Davis, Sam Simpson, Gary Roberson, Greg Roberson, Darnell Parker, Cheryl Jones, Cheryl LaCour, Robert and Orvette Walker, Adwin Brown, Michael Smith, Enrique Emil, Forrest Walton, Mark Armstrong, Dale and Phoebe Whyte, August Matia, Roberto Barnett, Troy Carr, Arlene Andrews, Keith Smith, Keith Ellison, Brian Mahoney, Fred Bradford, Jeff and LaSandra Hill, Nate and Leslie Cox, George Morton, Rob and Patricia Cannon, Darren Lee, Darryl Carter, Tom and Sandy Leander, Sean Carney, Enoch Simmons, Terrell Lawry, Mike Yost, Hank Gathers, Bo Kimble, Corey Gaines, Jeff Fryer, Russell and Lisa Ellis, Pastor Julius and Tina West, Irving and Dr. LaVern Tolbert, Lovey and Gwen Martin, Keisha Woods, Elgin and April Mosby, Darryl and Beatrice Howard, John and Odette Board, Craig and Carol Hart, Patricia Boyd, Latricia Crump, Harvey and LaTanya Lewis, Virgil Byars, Robert Lee, Dwyane Capers, Rodney Green, John Glenn Van Buren, Sterling and Tanya Lucas, John "Pete" Graham, Steve Thomas, David "Tex" Thomas, Maurice Palmer, Robert Mixon, Frank and Bunny Wilson, Pastor Sheridan and Larleslie Mc Daniel, Pastor Garrick and Felicia Huff, Pastor Demetris and Angela Miles, Valerie McDaniel, Pastor Dexter and Tanisha Robinson, Lane and Carol Cooper, Darren and Tinesia Mars, Larry and Chan Clark, Elic and

Natasha Mahone, Shaieda Prince, Tommy and Janice Boyd, Pastor Vernon and Yvette Mothershed, Kris and Latasha Thornton, Ron and Sharon Hill, Fred and Gladys Hill, Doris Pegues, Lori Pegues, Janet Cates, Carol Provo, Craig Parker, Tamika White, A.J. Luke, Gerald and Felicia Carmon, Troy and Regina Carmon, Eric and Donna Irvine, Michael and Alexis Gramling, Aldina Washington, Michael and Hope Davis, Sterling Hicks, Ken and Akida Lewis, Grandpa Ed and Ada Taylor, Dorothy Meacham, Troy Meacham, Baldwin and Ernestine Fisher, Edward and Bernice Taylor, Dennis Taylor, Lonnie Carter, Elmer Babe Wilson, George and Ola Carter, Art and Keisha Fisher, Cheryl Fisher, Eddie and Sonya Taylor, Corey Taylor, Brendon Taylor, Michelle Fisher, Anthony Boyd, Pat Boyd, Kenny Boyd, Deon Boyd, Paul Boyd, Kim Boyd, Cedric Farmer, Kenneth Farmer, Jerome Whitfield, Aaron Cox, Dwayne Stearns, Daryl Cameron, Mark Jones, Michael Byars, Jeff Joseph, Kevin Joseph, Terry Joseph, Joe Weakley, Paul Weakley, Wally Rank, Willard "Bubba" Scott, George Swain, Michael "Nudy" Carr, Michael Carr, Robert Graham, Karl Watson, Donald Young, Darren and Sonia Earley, William Broomfield, Donald and Terri Edwards, Pastor Charles and Carol Latchison, Deon and Dawn Reid, Coach Paul Westhead, Fr. Al Koppes, Prof. Kimberly Haag, Dr. Irene Oliver, Dr. Shane Martin, Gloria Davidson, Kay Duenas, Tangee Smith-Hill, Kevin and Shawn Cooperwood, Larry and Jackie Clark, Cynthia D. Terry, Darryl and Creasy Adams, Eric and LaKeisha Tillman, Jack and Sheryl Lightsy, Chris and Tracey Smith, Jose and Mary Ann Rodriguez, Cyndi Croad, Ernest and Dena Allen, Dirk and Treca Adams, Sharon Douglas, Pat Morgan, Shannon Morgan, Tara Fletcher, Cathy Marks, Dena Thomas, Ted and Traci Clapp, Mike Bohanan, Trina Jones, Greg and Tanya Burns, Andre and Trudy Montgomery, Dr. Darrel and Avis Hartley, Anita Birt, Keith Slice, Janet Martin, Karim and Kenitha Saafir, Kenneth Martin, Nate Gainous, Robert Williams, Sr., Georgia Beverly, Amber Whittaker, Candy Marsh, Brandy Marsh, Rachel Smith,

Crystal Wells, Janice Cain, Tyrone Randolph, Ghana and Antoinette Williams, Tracy Body, Natasha Ellis, Jennifer Jennings, Joanne Jenkins, Momma Faye Peoples, Tribrina Brown, Twylar Ventus, Cecilia Knott, Stacey Martin, Diedre Hope-Wheeler, Nekii Montgomery, La Shundra Johnson, Beverly Arnold, Chris and Lisa Wells, Lois Alacorn, Sam and Marcy Brown, Ann Saunders, Ursula Houston, Larry and Yolanda McDowell, Eddie and Pat Williams, Virgil Campbell, Carlette Wesley, Patsy Adams, James and Ann Williams, Roy Fegan, Alex Sansberry, Solomon Miller, Dr. Mardi Reese, Donna Thompson, Paul Scranton, Michael Dennis, Rhonita Thornton, Brian Bolden, Charles Morgan, Liz Seraphin, Dr. Robert Barner, Bill Bermudez, Janet Addo, Jim and Delores Golston, David Flores, Dr. Randy Ward, Mickey Cureton, Patrick Huff, Pastor Charles Bennett, Chris Washington, Dennis Schaffer, Robbie Henderson, Victor Forkland, Vann Scott, Eliza Haber, Ida Barnes, Bobby Walton, Von Sherri Barnes, David Brown, Drexel Brown, Darryl Brown, Dean Brown, Derrick Brown, Ronald Scipio, Joe Clark, Marshall and Trina Spates, Pastor Roderick and Nina Walker, Michael and Tracey Evans, Pastor Edward and Lenita Chung, Ricardo Wiggins, Eric and Carol Anderson, Frank Nelms, Ron Carter, Phillip and Janet Bailey, Rod Amos, Brian and Kay Bowen, Gwen Wykoff, Don and Michelle Mahoney, Jan Titus, Vivica Keyes, Pastor Edwina Harris, Joe and Precious Johnson, Betty De Cruz, Pastor Mary Jones, Suzette Mitchell, Lisa Hawkins, Don and Wintress Barnes, Karen Elaine Robinson, Fred and Karen Griffin, Fred and Margo Barrier, Laron and Halana Christopher, Yashica Patterson, Olivia Ellis, Keith and April Howze, Brett and Trina Mars, Stephanie Gainous, Annie Roberson, Michelle Wills, Rene Wells, Robert McMann, Adriane Brown, Michelle Jefferies, Sandra Bradley, Michelle Bruce, Natalie Harada, Johnny Brown, Byron Roberts, Dwayne Polee, Alan and Stacy Gobert, Cynthia Dawkins, Vernell Robinson, Fate and Myra Haygood, Earlene Williams, Gerald Shaw, Tammy Calderon, Beverly Carter, Jerome

Johnson, Nia Crenshaw, Bertha Burns, Ivan Harris, Octavious Wiley, Gerald and Brenda Porter, Harold and Lois McDaniel, Lamont Hughes, Andre Hughes, Ross Green, Reggie Carr, Tommy Price, Joanne Manning, Virgil Williams, Daryl Copes, Thyeris Mason, Karen Rhodes, Kathy Dean, Joey Gaskin, Gabriel Berhane, Carl Peterson, Kevin Cook, Joe MacFarland, Melvin Kidd, Ben Henderson, Stan Robinson, Latricia Brown, Ronald Nelson, Michael Stewart, Ray Cole, Rene Carpenter, Tony Scarbourgh, James Charles, Gregory Brandon, Yvonne Wheeler, Steve Neal, Angela Scruggs, Wanda Montgomery, Valerie Cole, Valerie McZeal, Tim Kornegay, Dr. Gary and Pat Kornegay, Zaven and Alla Madattian, Jose Rodriguez, Narcisco Hernandez, Grizleda Antillion, Al and Tammy Cannister, Belma and Tammy Johnson, TeiYana Smith, Terry Muse, Alicia Jordan, Keri Valentine, Teresa Beck, Regina Edwards, Ron Edwards, Robert and Donna Marshall, Edward and Gloria Marshall, Pastor Steve Dyson, Pastor Ahmed and Virginia Ali, Lety Vidal, Gris Vidal, Robert Andrade, Roberto Flores, Gerald Williams, Dr. Donald Cheek, Trent and Andy Gaston, Todd Slaughter, Brian and Sherea Riley, Darnell Slaughter, Rodney and Donna Middleton, Tony and Mozel Veil, Pastor Richard and Queen Esther Askew, Ricky Gadbury, Early Parsons, Richard and Cheryl Solomon, Magic Johnson, A.C. Green, Byron Scott, Coach Bob Yarnell, Royal Clayton, Royce Clayton, Tim Garret, D'Anthony Langston, Dan Melendez, Kurtis Miller, Brian Benbow, Sean Dunbar, The Angel City Links, Inc.(special thanks to all the ladies), Reggie and Terri Matthews, Lisa Bradford, Gladys Ross, Torean Ross, Trevon Ross, Laron and Victoria Kemp, Beatrice Lowe, Greg and Kay Thompson, Kim Lowe, James Thompson, Roy Cole, Michael Capers, Ethel Denham, Harry Denham, Johnny Roberson, Helen Durrah, Katie McClendon, Lashai Joshua, Jamaica Carter, Lavel Carter, Jalin Carter, Lenford Joshua, Lloyd Joshua, Jael Carter, Curtis Carter, Freddy Iverson Carter, Leo Jordan Carter, Bertha Williams, Roberta Woods, Frank and Debbie Carter, Lonnie Carter, Teddy Carter, Freddy

Carter, Cliff and Jackie Dawson, Mike Owens, Ed McCaulley, James Brown, Mark and Gladys McAllister, Roderick and Sharon Vines, Ceola K. Haley, Willie Pittman, Greg McClendon, Lenford Joshua, Brandon and Kelly Bailey, Michael and Sheila Brown, Tony and Belinda Calloway, Carolyn Jones, Dena Davis Island, Benjie Knox, Kennedy Dixon, Brian Kennedy, Dr. Marilyn Lezine, Kevin and Shawnse Neighbors, Pastor William and Kim Irving, Michelle Poche, Danny Birdsong, Priscilla Birdsong, Shawn Birdsong, Warren Birdsong, Danny Brassell, Lee and Barbara Shoag, Earl and Linda Griffith, Robin Stone, Yvette Perrodin, Renard and Lisa Foster, Nevel and Podina Brown, Velesta Collins, Jeanette Collins Hector, Aundre Russell, Tony and Gina Smith, Rondal Rollings, Tiny Lister, Angela Arbet, LaTanya Guyes, Monica Jackson, Tiffany White, Dianne Ros, Sherri Franklin, Willie Marie Robertson, John Bryant, Carolina Castorena, Chamika Smith, Dawn Lopez, Marco Duran, Juan Hernandez, Eydie Lopez, Latoya Wilson, Earl and Sheila Patterson, Yesenia Huesca, Maria Gutierrez, Estella Gutierrez, Latessi Burris, Marcus Egland, Tedrich Johnson, Eric Knox, Rick Sharp, Jackie Williams, Chester Perry, Ed and Wanetta Samuels, Andrew and Mary Buggs, William Gideon, Paul Hicks, Omar Montgomery, Kim Yates, Stephanie Dunn, Jennifer Rubin, Carol King, Melissa King, Reggie Moore, Anthony O'Dell (my little brother), Manny O'Dell, Mike and Rosemary Lopez, Arlene Conelly, Helen Satorius, Lester Logan, Denine Gardenhire, Adrianne Matte, Rebecca Gibson, Martha Frazier, Bill Hockerson, Les Wolf, Julie Johnson, Allison Henderson, Carolyn Terry, Kevin Provost, Dorie Gayner, Nancy Egelko, Roberta Crowson, Keith Ladd, Gary Maldanado, Herman Clayborn, Dr. Avery Hall, Adelmo Martinez, Dorothy Harper, Mel Collins, Judith McBride, Joan McBride, Shawn Ashley, Chris Cook, Lewis and Montorie Hodo, Linda Hodo-Haley, Lorie Hodo, Dezra White, Linda Moore, Diane Brown, Mike Zamora, Ernest Cash, Joslyn Zenon Smith, Clarence Evans, Katie Scott, Eva Dowdell,

Gloria N. Livas, Christine Hill, Mattie Fegan, Sylvia Owens, Emma Henderson, Lester and Rene McGee, Dr. Kristi Kahl, Rosalind Morgan, Georgetta McNeal, Wanda Oliver, Shawn Ashley, Beverly Charles, Denise "Sparkle" Peterson, Connie Jensen, Dr. Stephanie Holzman, Jim Saurez, Teresa Osburn, Mellow and Mary Beth Walker, Larita Shelby, Cindy Bowers, Eugene Obillo, Pastor Stephanie Douglas, Charles and Mia Reed, Lynn O'Hearn, Gladys Agredano, Vince and Pattie Smith, Karina Agredano, Eric and Toni Porter, Juwayne Jenkins, Bill and Ann Calhoun, Robbie Butler, Reggie Butler, Alvis Van Buren, Leon Annel, Bishop Gary McIntosh, Bishop Carlton Pearson, Pastor Davy Cobb, Dr. Miles Monroe, Bishop Kenneth C. Ulmer, Kurt Karr, Dawn Cannon, Bishop Charles Blake, Lee Douglas, Rod and Sharon Lamar, Pastor Rick Hawkins, Hank Waddles, all my brothers in Terminal Island F.C.I. and Taft F.C.I., the students from: Wilson Riles Elementary School, 107th Street Elementary School, Millikan High School, Lindberg Middle School, Hamilton Middle School, Loyola Marymount University, W.A.V.E. CEC, Manual Arts CEC, Crenshaw CEC, and Crenshaw CDS, T.K. Aaron-Lyday, Emmanuel and Henrietta Udenci, George Carter, Rodney and Kim Dodley, Wyking Jones, Pastor Ralph and Kathy Mosby, Michael Carradine, Tracey Robinson, Patrice Prothro, Jamie Bragg, Joe Haywood, Frank Jones, Thelonious Alexander, Leon Forte, Patricia Del Hagan, Carl Cohn, Kelley Hurley, Monica Daly, Valida Gory, Brenda Jefferson, Jercole Govan, Rodney and Tonette Taylor, Roger Wyatt, Randolph Simpson, Tiffany C'deBaca, John Alston, Ben Rico, Mike Malsbury, Gene Reitz, Michael and Claudinette Brown, Rhong Phin, Keisha Blanks, Umeka Robinson, Renee McAllister, and Karima A. Charles.